A Woman's Workshop on BIBLE MARRIAGES

D1569037

Books in this series—

A Woman's Workshop on BIBLE MARRIAGES

Leader's Manual

Diane Brummel Bloem
With Robert C. Bloem

ZONDERVAN PUBLISHING HOUSE   OF THE ZONDERVAN CORPORATION
GRAND RAPIDS, MICHIGAN 49506

A WOMAN'S WORKSHOP ON BIBLE MARRIAGES — Leader's Manual
Copyright © 1980 by The Zondervan Corporation
Grand Rapids, Michigan

ISBN 0-310-21401-7

All Scripture quotations are from the Holy Bible: New International Version, copyright © 1978 by the New York International Bible Society. Used by permission.

Printed in the United States of America

83 84 85 86 87 88 — 10 9 8 7 6 5 4

We lovingly dedicate this book
to our children,
Bill, Beth, and Mary,
praying that they each may know
the joys of a Christian marriage
as we know them

CONTENTS

ACKNOWLEDGMENTS

We thank the Reverend Leonard Greenway, Th.M., Th.D., for evaluating this manuscript and for his continuing encouragement.

We also thank Dick and Jacque Bolt, Harold and Gladys Kuipers, Stan and Carrie Sinnema for their insights as we studied these lessons in embryonic form with them.

Above all, we thank God for all He has taught us as we prepared this book. It is our prayer that those who use this book will glorify the Lord with us as we exalt His name together (Ps. 34:3).

PREFACE

We believe that every account of the lives of people included in the Bible is put there for a purpose. When we study the lives of Bible characters, we are amazed that problems, joys, and personality types have changed so little over the centuries. We see ourselves and many people we know.

This book does not attempt to explore each facet of a Bible person's life, but focuses on the *marriages* of these Bible people. Many factors (war or peace, poverty or prosperity, problems, spiritual commitment, disappointments, hopes, personalities) shape the course of a marriage. These factors are studied only as they affect the marriage. Every effort has been made to keep the lessons based on Bible facts and not on speculation. The lessons are not in chronological order because we believe a change of scene and time sustains interest. All quotations are from the New International Version of the Bible unless stated otherwise.

We are excited because God through the Holy Spirit has opened our eyes and our ears as we have worked on this material, and we think you too will be excited as you study these lessons. We must warn you, though, that preparation cannot be left to the last minute. The "Questions for Group Discussion" are dependent on the answers to the "Questions for Personal Study." Each participant should have his/her own student's manual. The leader should answer the student questions before reading the leader's manual. Some of these lessons may take two sessions depending on your method and the amount of discussion generated.

This is the way we wrote this book: Diane did the research and wrote the objectives, background material, and questions. Bob studied the Bible passages and worked out the answers to the questions. We then discussed the material, edited it, and revised it. Next, Diane wrote the Leader's Manual and Bob proofread and evaluated it. Studying and discussing this material together has greatly enriched our marriage. We have grown in love for the Lord and for each other.

In these marriage vignettes, God provides us with hindsight so we may see how He works. We see the outcome of events that shape a marriage, and we see how God regards these people and their lives. We believe God guides, warns, comforts, and encourages us as we study these people. This book goes out with much prayer that God will use it mightily to strengthen and encourage you, His children. May you who study it be led by the Holy Spirit and be blessed as we have been.

BOB AND DIANE BLOEM

1

MR. AND MRS. SIMON PETER

BIBLE PASSAGE

1 Peter 3:1–7

OBJECTIVES

1. To show that Peter was married.
2. To show that Peter's wife accompanied and helped him.
3. To explore the claims of marriage when God calls to special service.
4. To see how Peter's personality and experiences relate to the marital advice he gives.
5. To examine the marital advice in this passage.
   Note: Objectives are listed in the order they are discussed in the lesson.

BACKGROUND

Simon Peter, the impetuous apostle, was a fisherman on the Sea of Galilee before Jesus called him to special service. He was one of the three disciples closest to Jesus and the only one who attempted to defend Him (John 18:10–11). Yet Peter, who had confessed, "You are the Christ, the Son of the living God" (Matt. 16:16), denied the Lord three times and then wept bitter tears of repentance. The Lord restored him threefold (John 21:15–19) and gave him a special pastoral charge. Peter was the spokesman for the group at Pentecost and a fearless leader in the early church. He feared only one thing—other people—and Paul admonished him for this (Gal. 2:11–14).

This very human man had a wife. We learn about her only through inference, so we cannot study her personality. We can, however, study their marriage with Peter as its representative and spokesman.

QUESTIONS FOR PERSONAL STUDY

1. *How do we know that Peter was married (Mark 1:30)?* He had a mother-in-law.
2. *What are Peter's names (John 1:40–42)?* Simon, Cephas (Aramaic), and Peter (Greek). This question is included so that the student will understand that "Cephas" in 1 Corinthians 9:5 is Peter.
3. *What does 1 Corinthians 9:5 tell us about Mrs. Peter's spiritual commitment and participation in her husband's work?* The NIV translates this verse: "Don't we have the right to take a believing wife along with us, as do the other apostles and the Lord's brothers and Cephas?" This tells us that Peter's wife was a believer and accompanied him in his work.
4. *What was Peter's occupation (Matt. 4:18–20)?* He was a fisherman so he was probably not rich. He became a

"fisher of men" which took him away from home for days and weeks at a time.

5. *Did Peter forsake his wife to follow Jesus (Mark 1:29–30, 35–37)?* Peter's wife may have felt lonely and forsaken when Peter was away for long periods of time. She was not alone, though, because her mother was with her. She was not forsaken either because Peter stayed at home when he was in town.

   Their home was in Capernaum (Mark 1:21). Jesus also had a home there (Mark 4:13) and performed many miracles there. In that city He healed the centurion's servant (Matt. 8:5–13), the paralyzed man who was let down through the roof (Mark 2:1–12), and the official's son (John 4:46–54). This last He did while on His way home from Cana. In fact, He did so many wonderful things in Capernaum that people of other cities were envious (Luke 4:23). Jesus also held Capernaum especially responsible to believe in Him (Matt. 11:20–24). He taught at great length there (John 6:59) and visited there on other occasions (Matt. 17:24; John 2:12; 6:16–17, 24). From this we conclude that Capernaum was home base for Jesus and His disciples. Peter's wife was not forsaken. She "kept the home fires burning" and perhaps accompanied Peter even then.

6. *Does Jesus demand that His followers forsake husband or wife to serve Him (Matt. 19:4–6, 27–30)?* In this chapter (vv. 4–6), Jesus stresses the indissoluble union of husband and wife and denounces divorce. He would not be responsible for the destruction of a marriage.

7. *What can we infer about Mrs. Peter's life and kingdom service from Mark 1:29–35; 1 Corinthians 9:5; and (possibly) 1 Peter 5:13?* A great crowd followed Jesus and often needed provisions. Peter (1 Peter 4:9) stresses hos-

pitality as a Christian virtue, and evidently he and his wife practiced it in their home. This would have kept his wife very busy and involved in his work. We assume that she assisted him when she accompanied him in his work. Some commentators believe Peter's wife joined him in sending greetings in 1 Peter 5:13.

8. *What do we know about Peter's temperament and experiences?* He was impulsive and bold. He walked on the water until his faith failed (Matt. 14:28–31). He dared to rebuke Jesus, who then rebuked him (Matt. 16:22–23). He spoke before he thought. He was chosen to experience the Transfiguration of Jesus (Mark 9:5–6). He didn't want Jesus to serve him until he realized he wouldn't belong to Jesus unless Jesus washed him. Then he accepted and wanted to be completely washed (John 13:6–9). He took the lead and told John to ask Jesus for the name of the betrayer (John 13:24). He had great self-confidence and thought he was willing to lay down his life for Jesus (John 13:36–38). He was the only one who tried to defend Jesus (John 18:10–11). His bravado crumbled before a servant girl, and he denied Jesus three times. He wept bitterly (Luke 22:54–62). He ran to the tomb. He did everything with energy (Luke 24:12). When Jesus reinstated the humbled Peter, he was eager to declare his love for the Lord and was hurt because Jesus asked him three times. He felt so close to Jesus that he dared to ask about John's future since Jesus had just prophesied about Peter's (John 21:15–23). He was unschooled, ordinary, but was equipped with courage and ability because he had been with Jesus and had received the Holy Spirit (Acts 4:13). In obedience to God, he fearlessly proclaimed the gospel (Acts 4:18–20).

9. *After reading 1 Peter 3:1–7, do you get the impression*

that Peter was a harsh, demanding husband? This is a subjective question so answers will vary. Peter seems to be mainly interested in an orderly, harmonious home. We have explored his personality and temperament a bit. He seems to me to be the type of person who would resent a wife who chided or reproached him. Perhaps his wife realized that he would explode if treated so and thus developed an influential, inner Christian beauty. I get the feeling Peter appreciated this and has her in mind as a lovely "daughter of Sarah."

10. *Why does Peter exhort wives to be submissive?* His main reason in this passage is to create a home climate in which the Spirit can make the husband receptive to the gospel message. Peter obviously agrees with Paul's writings on the headship of the husband in marriage. (See Eph. 5:22–23).

11. *Does this apply only to wives of unbelieving husbands?* Peter broadens the scope when he uses Sarah, the wife of a believing husband, as an example.

12. *Why would a man's prayers be hindered if he did not live considerately with his wife (1 Peter 3:7)?* A man who does not treat his wife well is not Christlike. He exalts himself and his wishes, treating her as inferior or unequal. Peter points out that husband and wife are equally "joint heirs" (RSV) of eternal life. A husband who mistreats his wife is not carrying out the protective role God has assigned to him. Unforgiven sin of any sort—and this is sin—builds a wall of separation between man and God.

QUESTIONS FOR GROUP DISCUSSION

1. *On the basis of what you have learned about Peter from his life and advice, describe him as a husband.* If possi-

ble, let several group members respond to this question. Peter must have been a dashing, exciting, exasperating young husband. As he grew older and learned to be submissive to his Lord, I imagine he became more patient, understanding, and appreciative. He might have embarrassed his wife on occasion, but I believe he was a tower of strength for her.

My husband sees Peter as a loving husband who needed his wife as a helper in his work and wanted her to be a devoted Christian. He sees Peter's love for his wife expressed in his concern for her mother.

2. *Paul states rather enviously that Peter and other leaders in the early church had their wives accompany them in their work (1 Cor. 9:5). He also suggests that those who would serve Christ devotedly should not marry (1 Cor. 7:32–35). How would a mate be a help or a hindrance to a church leader?* Many examples can be given. To start, it may be pointed out that a mate's poor health, desire for material goods, or untrustworthiness could hinder a person's work for the Lord. On the other hand, one's mate may be alert to needs of others and to the needs of his or her spouse, to undercurrents in the church, etc., and thus increase the effectiveness of the person's work.

3. *If a Christian husband or wife feels called to Christian service, such as on the mission field, must his or her mate be equally committed to this calling? Explain.* In my opinion, a married couple must be agreed and equally committed to the cause of Christ they are serving if they are to be effective. Amos 3:3 states: "Do two walk together unless they have agreed to do so?" This verse is in a section which points out that "the Sovereign Lord does nothing without revealing his plan to his servants the prophets" (v. 7). God shows us by His own example that

communication with and commitment to one another is essential in carrying on His work.

Matthew 18:19 may also be used to answer this question: "Again, I tell you that if two of you on earth agree about anything you ask for, it will be done for you by my Father in heaven." A husband and wife united in work and prayer are powerful.

My husband adds, "Less than total support for one another on the mission field would create only strife and hurt the cause of Christ. This is also true off the mission field."

4. *What is the submission Peter calls for in 1 Peter 3:1 to be like?* In 1 Peter 2:13, 18; 3:1, 7–9 Peter is recalling the submission taught and practiced by Jesus. These verses cause us to review the Sermon on the Mount (Matt. 5–7), remembering such phrases as "Going the second mile" (Matt. 5:41).

This submission calls for a wife to work energetically, lovingly, intelligently, and creatively with her husband to build a loving, Christian marriage and home. It requires her to recognize his authority and headship and to accept his final decision if things have been discussed and there is not complete agreement between husband and wife.

5. *What is not called for in the submissive role of wives?* Submission does not call for a wife to be an unthinking doormat, nor does it allow husbands to be unkind and unjust. It does not allow a wife to take a helpless, apathetic attitude. She is, after all, to be her husband's helper (Gen. 2:18). Group members may have many more ideas and examples to share.

6. *Did Peter know anything about submission? Explain.* As we have seen (question 8 above), Peter had to learn to recognize the headship of Jesus. He may have been older

than Jesus, making this difficult to accept. As he learned to submit to Christ, the head of the church, Peter became more effective in his ministry.

7. *Peter uses the word "likewise" in 1 Peter 3:1, 7 RSV ("in the same way" NIV). To what is he referring? (See 1 Peter 2:21–25 and Phil. 2:4–8.)* Our submission is to be like Christ's, who did not put Himself first but in love was willing to suffer injustice for our salvation. He was willing to serve, and we should be willing to do the same.

8. *Since wives are exhorted to be submissive to husbands, should the word "obey" be included in the marriage vows? Explain.* I had no hesitation in promising to obey my husband because we both serve and obey the same Master. Today, however, many couples feel it is degrading for wives to promise to obey their husbands and are rewriting the marriage vows to exclude this word. My husband prefers emphasis on the word "love." For a Christian, love includes obedience to God and His Word and therefore of wives to husbands. Bob believes that since the word "obey" implies unreasoning submission or suggests tyranny, it is better to begin marriage by amplifying Christ's teaching on love.

Group members may wish to explore the reasons why the word "obey" evokes such negative thoughts. Perhaps other wordings could be suggested which are in agreement with the biblical call for wives to be submissive to their husbands (Eph. 5:21–33).

9. *Why doesn't Peter use the word "love" instead of "be considerate" in 1 Peter 3:7?* In Peter's day, as in ours, "love" meant many things and could easily be misinterpreted. The words "be considerate" are more specific and applicable to all the details and decisions in daily life.

My husband comments, "I think that as a lover and a husband Peter knew the thoughts of men, that if he had said 'love your wives' men would first think of sex. He wanted them to understand that in true love there must be consideration of the wife in all aspects of marriage—including sex."

10. *What is involved in living considerately with one another?* I think first of Solomon's wise words in Proverbs 24:3-4, "By wisdom a house is built, and through understanding it is established; through knowledge its rooms are filled with rare and beautiful treasures." In order for a husband and wife to live considerately with one another, they must know and understand one another. They must communicate. This is often hard work, but it is always worth the effort. When a husband and wife understand each other, they are through love able to put up with many irritations, and they can work together for peace and harmony and growth in their marriage. Bob adds, "If we talk things over, we don't just take over."

11. *Does Peter place a heavier burden on the husband or on the wife in working for a good marriage and harmonious home?* In many ways this depends on the character and personality of the people involved. It may involve suffering for either husband or wife. Some wives may find submission comforting and even delightful, while others feel their leadership abilities are ignored or stunted by it. Some husbands may enjoy headship while others lack confidence or initiative.

Bob believes that Peter is challenging wives to be peacemakers in the home—often a difficult job. Many women will agree and testify that their attitudes and actions set the "tone" of their family's life. It takes special wisdom and grace for a woman who has a strong personality or character traits to discipline herself and work for peace and harmony.

I believe Peter places a heavier burden on the husband than on the wife because he makes him ultimately responsible as head of the house. This is borne out in Ephesians 5:22–33 where a husband's role and task are compared with Christ's role as Head of the church.

12. *Were Mr. and Mrs. Simon Peter happily married?* We believe they were. They were united in the Lord.

2

ABRAHAM AND SARAH

BIBLE PASSAGES

Genesis 11–23 (specifically: Genesis 11:27–32; 12; 15; 16; 17:15–27; 18:1–15; 20; 21:1–13; 23; 25:7–11); Romans 4; Hebrews 11:8–12; 1 Peter 3:1–7

OBJECTIVES

1. To examine their response to God's call.
2. To consider their faith and doubts and to see how God dealt with them in both.
3. To understand their frustration while waiting for God to fulfill His promise.
4. To study the effect of the Hagar and Ishmael episode on their marriage.
5. To discuss today's alternatives to childlessness.
6. To analyze Sarah's obedience to Abraham.
7. To consider whether we should be active in working out God's plan.
8. To learn how we should decide on major moves or changes in our lives.

9. To be encouraged by the fact that God works through His
   friends—weak, human believers who are given the gift of
   faith.
   *Note: This lesson, which is necessarily long, may be
   studied in two sessions.*

BACKGROUND

Civilization progressed rapidly in some parts of the world
that were resettled after the Flood and the confusion of speech
at Babel. Many people know about the advanced culture of
Egypt where the art of writing was well-established more than
a thousand years before Abraham was born. The sophisti-
cated culture of Ur of the Chaldees is not as well-known.

Several locations have been suggested as the site of ancient
Ur. Because it is apparent that Abraham lived in a well-
established city about two thousand years before Christ, a site
excavated by archeologists in southern Iraq (once known as
Babylonia) seems most likely to have been Abraham's early
home.

Archeological work has revealed that perhaps a quarter of a
million people lived in metropolitan Ur. These people had
advanced systems of writing and mathematics. Their libraries
contained detailed records of educational, religious, and
business establishments. They had dictionaries, ency-
clopedias, and textbooks on various subjects. Beautiful art
objects have been found in the royal cemetery.

The people of Ur, though descendants of Noah's son Shem,
did not practice the true worship of God. There is archeological evidence of human sacrifice. From Joshua 24:2, 14 we
learn that Abraham's family served idols as did others in Ur.
However, the assertion of some authors that Terah, Abra-

ham's father, was a chief idol maker or leader of idol worship is unwarranted. If Abraham's family in Ur had been completely pagan and untouched by the call of God, there would have been no religious reason for Abraham to send his servant to his relatives to get a wife for Isaac. Laban and Bethuel's answer (Gen. 24:50–51) supports our conclusion that Abraham's family was blessed and called to the knowledge of the true God through Abraham's call.

God chose to call Abraham and Sarah out of the culture of Ur, and He promised them a rich inheritance, many descendants, and the prospect that all nations would be blessed through them.

QUESTIONS FOR PERSONAL STUDY

1. *Why did God want Abraham and Sarah to leave Ur (Gen. 11:31; Neh. 9:7; Acts 7:2–4) and Haran (Gen. 12:1–5)?*
   Among the answers that may be given are these:
   — God wanted to test Abraham's faith and commitment.
   — Their relationship with the true God could grow better away from the pagan culture of Ur.
   — This was the beginning of the separate, model nation God had planned from which the Messiah was to come.

2. *Were Abraham and Sarah both believers (Heb. 11:8, 11)?*
   They are set forth as heroes of faith in this Hebrews passage. Sarah and Rahab are the only women mentioned by name in this "Hall of Faith." As we study this lesson and become increasingly aware of their doubts and faults, we are amazed that Abraham and Sarah were so like us and yet were recognized and honored as among the greatest believers in Bible history.

3. *What hardships did they suffer by leaving Ur and becoming nomads?* The background material in this lesson suggests that it was a great sacrifice (from an earthly point of view) to leave the advanced culture of Ur. They left financial security, educational opportunities, friends, and family.

In her book *God Speaks to Women Today,* Eugenia Price points out that part of the trial lay in the fact that they did not have "the solace of being able to say, 'In three months or three years we will reach our destination and this will end.'"[1]

Instead, they packed their portable goods and set out for a nomadic life in the dry, windswept plains and wilderness. God promised to give them the land, but it was already occupied and experiencing famine—another test of their faith.

4. *How did God compensate for these hardships?* Bob answers, "He blessed them with His constant assurance that He was their God (Gen. 17:8)." He made them very wealthy, and He even preserved Sarah's remarkable beauty. Through these hardships He also gave them great spiritual growth. They learned to depend completely on God.

5. *What does it take to move out and not know where you are going (Heb. 11:8)?* Bob says, "It takes faith in God that He will bless you and open new doors of service to Him. If we face such a challenge today, without direct revelation from God, we must be sure that God—and not merely our own adventurous spirit—is directing us. Then we too can set out in faith as pioneers and missionaries have done for centuries."

[1]Eugenia Price, *God Speaks to Women Today* (Grand Rapids: Zondervan Publishing House, 1964), p. 18.

6. *What do you learn from Genesis 15:5–9 about God's patience in teaching His children?* Bob answers, "He took Abraham by the hand, as it were, and used a vivid example to explain the promise to him. He illustrated His commitment to Abraham." These verses inspire us to worship as we see our God as the patient, understanding Father and the gentle, creative Teacher.

We can follow our heavenly Father's example and learn to teach our children and students lovingly and effectively.

Looking at Abraham's simple, childlike belief and God's evaluation of it, we can examine ourselves, put away earthbound arguments and reasonings, and believe. This reminds us of Jesus' words in Matthew 18:3, "I tell you the truth, unless you change and become like little children, you will never enter the kingdom of heaven."

7. *Abraham and Sarah both laughed when God renewed His promise (Gen. 17:17; 18:12–15). Did they laugh for the same reason?* Many authors point to their laughter and charge them with doubt and unbelief. Jill Briscoe in *Prime Rib and Apple* presents Sarah as an arguing, contentious woman who even argued with God in her "raucous laugh of doubt."[2]

We discussed this laughter and agree that since God did not denounce Abraham and Sarah for the sin of unbelief, this was probably more of a self-conscious, embarrassed laughter. It certainly seemed impossible that they would have a child, and their laughter prompted God to remind them of His power in the words, "Is anything too hard for the Lord?" (Gen. 18:14). Yet, they are honored in Scripture for their implicit faith, so we prefer

---

[2]Jill Briscoe, *Prime Rib and Apple* (Grand Rapids: Zondervan Publishing House, 1976), p. 34.

to think that their laughter was prompted by staggering belief. The time for fulfillment had finally come, and their response was, "I can hardly believe it! What will people think?"

Did God punish them for laughing? No.

Did this disqualify them as "heroes of faith" (Heb. 11:8–12)? Note also Romans 4:20. No.

What may we conclude from this? Bob sees encouragement in this, and so do I. He feels that God provides laughter in the face of human impossibility. We can laugh with joy, incredulity, and even in embarrassment as we see God work the impossible. God understands because He reads our hearts, "he knows how we are formed; he remembers that we are dust" (Ps. 103:14), and He forgives our sins. Praise His name!

8. *Did Abraham lie when he claimed Sarah as his sister (Gen. 12:13; 20:2, 12)?* People married close relatives in those days, and according to 20:12, Sarah was his half-sister. Abraham did not really lie, but he did not tell the whole truth.

   Whether Abraham was cowardly or resourceful in this matter is debatable. It is an example of humans using their own wits to see them through a dangerous situation and thus exposing themselves to even more danger. What would have been the results if Sarah had been violated by Pharaoh or Abimelech? Praise God who controls all things! He guarded His promise and preserved them from harm. More than that, He made them rich and notable and demonstrated His power through their weakness.

9. *Did Abraham demand or request Sarah's obedience?* He requested it. He said, "This is how you can show your love to me" (Gen. 20:13).

10. *Should Sarah have obeyed him in this matter?* We looked at this from their finite viewpoint. They knew the danger. They believed Abraham had to be kept alive so the promise could be fulfilled. They loved each other. It was "only a white lie." Sarah was not lying to protect Abraham from some deserved punishment.

    They used their human resources just as we do; they forgot the tremendous divine resources available to them. Ideally, Sarah should have reminded her husband to call on God and to trust Him to preserve them. As Peter charges wives, "Do what is right and do not give way to fear" (1 Peter 3:6).

11. *Did Sarah blame God for her barrenness (Gen. 16:2)?* Bob says, "I don't think she blamed Him in anger, but confessed that God has the power to give and withhold children." I hear a sad note here. Sarah felt keen disappointment and hurt because she believed the Lord had rejected her as mother of the promised child.

12. *Give at least two possible motives for her offering Hagar to Abraham (Gen. 16:1–2).* We thought of several:
    — She loved her husband and wanted him to have the blessings of parenthood.
    — In those days marriage contracts required the wife to provide a child as heir or else to employ a substitute to bear a child for her.
    — She may have been tired of bearing the social stigma and pressure of being childless.
    — She did not see how God could fulfill the promise through her aging body so she assumed she had been rejected.
    — She believed "God helps those who help themselves." This is often quoted by people who think it is a biblical proverb. It is not.

13. *Was this easy for her to do?* It must have been a most painful decision—as though she were sacrificing herself. Abraham had demonstrated his love for Sarah by keeping her as his wife through all the years of waiting for a child. In those days, a sterile wife was divorced. We believe Sarah acted out of love and frustration and that she trusted Abraham to keep his commitment to her and not agree to a surrogate mother for carnal reasons or sexual pleasure.

14. *Should Abraham have been stronger and rejected her suggestion?* It is easy to judge Sarah and Abraham from our vantage point. They were caught in a web of circumstances and emotions. We can learn from their experience: they should not have acted before consulting God and being assured that this was His answer. So often we, too, act hastily before we are sure of the Lord's leading.

15. *Why didn't Abraham want to send Hagar and Ishmael away (Gen. 21:8–14)?* It is easy to understand Abraham's reluctance to send his own child away without any inheritance. He loved Ishmael. Both Abraham and Ishmael had been circumcised when Ishmael was thirteen years old, and this had bound them together under the sign of the covenant (Gen. 17:26). Then, too, we have a record of Abraham's prayer, "If only Ishmael might live under your blessing!" (Gen. 17:18), which expressed his love and concern for Ishmael. Add to this the fact that custom and law of that day forbade the expulsion of a slave wife and her children, and his reluctance is understandable. God comforted Abraham by taking Fatherly responsibility for Ishmael (Gen. 21:13; 17:20).

16. *Why did Sarah want them to go?* In this case, Sarah was given wisdom and was used of God to prompt the painful decision to remove all competition with Isaac as the chosen heir.

17. *What qualities in their lives drew Abraham and Sarah together?* These are some of the possible answers:
    — Their faith in God.
    — Their concern over their childlessness.
    — Their common background and family ties.
    — Their life as wanderers and nomads.
    — Their rescue by God in times of danger.
18. *What factors would tend to separate them?*
    — Abraham may have resented the dangers occasioned by Sarah's beauty, while she may have resented his willingness for her to be taken as a king's concubine.
    — Their frustration over childlessness could have caused them to blame each other.
    — Sarah's jealousy of Hagar and Abraham's love for Ishmael caused problems (Gen. 16:4–6; 21:11).
19. *Did Abraham consider Sarah his equal? Explain.* First Peter 3:1–7 presents Sarah as a model wife who submitted to her husband. Some people see this as license for a husband to rule oppressively and even cruelly over his "inferior" wife. This conclusion may not be drawn from the marriage of Abraham and Sarah and is not supported by the rest of the Bible.

    Abraham consulted his wife and requested her to agree with him out of love (Gen. 12:13; 20:13). He shared equally with her in the duties of hospitality (Gen. 18:6–8). When they had problems with Hagar, he gave Sarah control of the situation and ultimately acknowledged the rightness of her decision that Hagar and Ishmael must be sent away (Gen. 16:6; 21:12). Abraham loved Sarah and mourned her death, securing her burial place as his one purchased parcel of ground in the Promised Land (Gen. 23).

Abraham and Sarah were equally honored by God for their faith (Heb. 11:8–12), and they were equally declared righteous through faith (Rom. 4:5, Gal. 3:25–29). In the marriage relationship, though, God has established the husband as head to bear the most responsibility and authority. This is beautifully and tenderly taught in Ephesians 5:21–33, and it is this type of marriage relationship that Peter challenges us to emulate.

QUESTIONS FOR GROUP DISCUSSION

1. *If a man is called by God to transfer to another job or move to another place, should he consult his wife before he decides to go?* First, when God calls, we must answer yes or risk His judgment on us. A husband who cannot say yes to God without his wife's permission has placed her desires above God's will for his life.

   Second, in a good Christian marriage, a husband and wife discuss and pray about all major decisions so they can follow God's will together. In this respect, the answer would be yes. God does not speak to us in direct revelation today, so it would be wise to consult one another, count the cost, and determine God's will together.

   Third, God would not call one partner to do something that would truly injure the other. However, the call might require pain and sacrifice on the part of one or both mates.

   At first glance, this question may seem to apply mostly to business transfers, but it may be applied to entering missionary work or enlisting in the army or other commitments. Bob's father, who is now eighty-eight years old, often recalls his painful decision to volunteer as a soldier in World War I, leaving his young, pregnant wife alone and poverty-stricken. He still believes he made the right decision, but he is amazed that they were able to make the decision and then live through the trial without knowing for sure that they would be happily reunited. They were both Christians and were sustained by God's grace.

2. *Why was it so wonderful to be the father of a great nation? Would such a promise motivate you to set out on a journey in faith?* The promise to Abraham was three-dimensional. In short-term fulfillment God promised Abraham land and a son. In the future, perhaps beyond his life expectancy, God promised him many descendants and a great name. In the far distant future, God promised that all the families of the earth would be blessed through Abraham.

Today many people are choosing not to have children. Our society seems obsessed with immediate gratification in all areas of life: sex before marriage, credit purchases, etc. A promise that would not be realized until after death would not motivate many.

Then, too, we seem to be more interested in our own material possessions than in blessings to all the families of the earth. Bob and I feel that true soul-searching reveals that as a society we are self-seeking and sick.

Your discussion group may wish to analyze these trends and ask if Christians should take affirmative action to change them. They may also consider a possible spiritual fulfillment of the promise to Abraham and to us today, i.e., a desire by Christians to bring the gospel to many, thus obtaining many spiritual children who will be used to bless the whole earth (1 Cor. 4:14–17). This is one way in which we can claim the promise made to our spiritual father Abraham and his descendants (Rom.

4:13–17). The emphasis of any study of Abraham and Sarah must focus upon the promise of salvation through Christ who came through their family line centuries after they set out in faith.

3. *Why did God make Abraham and Sarah wait so long before He fulfilled His promise?* We suggest these possible reasons:

— He tested their faith and taught them patience.
— They had to grow spiritually to be ready for this great blessing.
— God waited until it was humanly impossible for Sarah to conceive so that God would be praised for doing the impossible. (Compare Isaac's conception with Christ's.)
— God wanted to call attention to this child so that the world would watch to see what God would do through him.

4. *Does Peter praise Sarah for obeying her husband's request to lie for him (Gen. 12:13; 20:2; 1 Peter 3:5–6)?* (See answers to 9, 10, and 19 of Questions for Personal Study.) I agree with Bob who sees the words in 1 Peter as referring to Sarah's recognition of her husband's authority over her in the marriage relationship. We believe the emphasis here lies on "do what is right and do not give way to fear." This may mean wives are not to fear their husbands' authority but are to honor it as right. It may refer to Sarah's confronting Abraham and asking him to send Hagar and Ishmael away (Gen. 21:10–11). In a contemporary setting, Peter's words call Christian women to dare to do right, to submit to their husbands' authority, and not to be intimidated by those who claim that equality of men and women repeals this command to be submissive in marriage.

5. *Was it wrong for Abraham and Sarah to go to Egypt in time of famine (Gen. 12:10)? Should they have stayed in the Promised Land and trusted God to provide?* Bob points out that God did not openly rebuke them for their move as they were using their God-given intelligence to cope with a difficult problem. I believe that ideally they should have stayed in the Promised Land and trusted or perhaps sent servants to buy grain, but they were young in faith and had to grow in trust as all God's children must do. When they entered another pagan culture, they were in physical and spiritual danger. Later Isaac became enmeshed in the same type of problem (Gen. 26:1–11). Jacob and his family did well so long as they stayed in the Promised Land and sent family representatives to Egypt to buy food (Gen. 42:1–5), but when they moved there, they became trapped in slavery (Exod. 1:8–14). Elimelech and Naomi were absorbed by a pagan culture when they moved to Moab during Bethlehem's famine. The sorrows that resulted made Naomi bitter (Ruth 1:1–5, 19–21).

We believe we may conclude that it is right to act and to act in faith, but it is not right to jeopardize spiritual growth or purity for the sake of providing for material needs.

6. *Does this lesson have any application for today when the trend is for childless couples to resort to adoption, artificial insemination, "test-tube" babies, or surrogate mothers?* Even today, many childless couples are crying out to God for the blessing of children. The above options are becoming available to most families in the Western world. The interesting case history of a couple who chose to have a baby by a surrogate mother was published in the article "The Gift Child" by Judith Ram-

sey in the 18 September 1979 issue of *Family Circle* magazine, page 70.

With spiritual hindsight we see that Abraham and Sarah did not consult God for approval of their plan to use Hagar as a surrogate mother. Couples must seek God's guidance and must be certain they are following His will for them when they decide to obtain a child through the use of exceptional means. Then the child God gives them will truly be a blessing.

7. *Why did God agree with Sarah in Genesis 21:8–14?* Sarah knew that if Hagar and Ishmael did not go, Isaac, the younger son, would not be established as the heir to Abraham's spiritual and material wealth. Isaac had to receive the birthright blessing because he was the promised child, God's miracle child.

8. *What may we conclude from this for marriages today?* Bob points out that in families with children from two different mothers there is rivalry and competiton for the father's affection. It takes special grace to have a peaceful and harmonious household under these conditions. God solved the problem for Abraham by separating his two families. Any couples contemplating a marriage involving two families of children should pray for and use special wisdom before and after making such a decision.

9. *Are today's troubles in the Mideast a result of this attempt of Abraham and Sarah to "help" God keep His promise?* The nucleus of people who began the Christless religion of Mohammedanism were descendants of Ishmael. They are still fighting with the descendants of Isaac for possession of the land promised to their father Abraham.

10. *In what ways may we be guilty of "running before the Lord"?* Many times we make quick, impulsive, or impatient decisions. Many times we manipulate events to

achieve a selfish end. Many times we rely on our own strength and intelligence to solve problems instead of asking and expecting God to act on our behalf.

11. *As Christian couples, would our marriages be healthier and happier if we separated ourselves more from secular culture?* In discussing this, group members may wish to consider the impact of television, movies, etc. on the mores and morals of people today. They may wish to compare marital stability and happiness of Christians in the mainstream of society with members of Amish, Mennonite, or other culturally separate groups.

12. *How should Christian couples make decisions to move, change jobs, etc.?* These matters should be decided with much prayer, a determination of God's will through His Word, and a good knowledge of all the facts involved. These matters should be decided with faith and without fear. Sometimes security is a hindrance to spiritual growth.

13. *God worked out His plan of salvation through weak human beings. Does He work in the same way today? Explain.* We look at our weak selves, prone to temptation and doubt, and we marvel that God calls us His friends (John 15:15) and is active today in our lives, working in us and through us. We praise God for this lesson that has revealed to us God's patience, His love, His bountiful goodness. Our faith may fail, but God's promises never fail! Praise His name!

3

AQUILA AND PRISCILLA

BIBLE PASSAGES

Acts 18:1–3, 18–19, 24–28; Romans 16:3–5; 1 Corinthians 16:19; 2 Timothy 4:19

OBJECTIVES

1. To study the friendship of Paul, Aquila, and Priscilla.
2. To study Priscilla and Aquila's "togetherness."
3. To discuss the possible spiritual leadership of Priscilla in the light of other Bible passages.
4. To observe the service rendered by Aquila and Priscilla and to examine it as a model for couples today.

BACKGROUND

About A.D. 50 Aquila and Priscilla were forced to leave their home in Rome because they were Jews and the emperor Claudius had decreed that all Jews must leave the city. This was not the first move for Aquila who was a native of Pontus (northern Turkey). It is not known why he emigrated to Rome. Some speculate that he was taken there as a slave and later freed. Others believe that he went there because the tent business flourished in Rome. Many commentators point out that his name, a Roman name, means "eagle" which could indicate that he came from a family of leaders having business dealings in several countries.

Much discussion has been generated by Priscilla's name. Priscilla was the diminutive form of the proper name Prisca, also a Roman name. Prisca means "venerable" or "ancient." This is taken by some to mean that she came from an old and noble Roman family. We do know that instead of calling her Prisca, the apostle Paul usually called her by the more endearing "Priscilla," which can be translated as "little old lady." This would be like calling an Elizabeth "Betsy." This reveals the closeness, the "family feeling," between Paul and Aquila and Priscilla.

QUESTIONS FOR PERSONAL STUDY

1. *What nationality was Aquila (Acts 18:2)?* Aquila was a Jew. Paul had the policy of preaching the gospel to the Jews of a community before going to the Gentiles (Rom. 1:16). He met Aquila when they were both newcomers in Corinth.

2. *Why had Priscilla and Aquila come to Corinth (Acts 18:2)?* Some historians, studying the writings of Suetonius, believe the Jewish sector of Rome was so disturbed by the introduction of Christianity that the peace of the city was endangered. The emperor Claudius tried to calm things down by ordering all the Jews to leave Rome. At this point in history, Corinth was a large Roman

colony with a large population of free Greeks, Romans, and Jews.

3. *What common bond did they have with Paul (Acts 18:3)?* They were all Jews and newcomers to Corinth, and they were all tentmakers. Responsible Jewish fathers always taught their children a trade so they would not be beggars or thieves. Paul boasted about his policy of self-support as a tentmaker and a missionary. You may read about this in 1 Corinthians 4:12; 9:6–15. These interesting verses help us to understand why Paul was drawn into a partnership and living arrangement with Aquila and Priscilla, getting to know them well as he worked and lived with them.

4. *What cities did Aquila and Priscilla live and serve in (Acts 18:1–2, 19; Romans 16:3–5)?* If we follow the travels of this couple, we see that they moved from Rome to Corinth, from Corinth to Ephesus, from Ephesus to Rome (Paul greets them in his letter to the Romans), and then, apparently, they moved back to Ephesus. We draw this conclusion after observing that Paul's last letter, 2 Timothy, was written from Rome, where he was imprisoned and about to be put to death, and in it he asks Timothy, who was serving in and near Ephesus, to come to him quickly and to greet Aquila and Priscilla (2 Tim. 4:6–22).

5. *What do we learn about them in Romans 16:5 and 1 Corinthians 16:19?* Congregations of the early church did not have church buildings; they met in the homes of believers. Wherever they lived, Aquila and Priscilla opened their home for worship services.

6. *How do you think they may have risked their lives for Paul (see Acts 18:12; 19:29–30)?* While most early Christians experienced danger and persecution, Paul got himself into some very tight spots. These verses show how his friends were involved and endangered with him

and how they restrained him. Bob points out that anyone who lived with Paul was endangered by the anger of the mobs who were against him.

7. *How were Aquila and Priscilla qualified to teach the learned Apollos (Acts 18:24–28)? See Acts 1:8; Philippians 4:9; 2 Timothy 2:2.* Perhaps the most interesting glimpse of Aquila and Priscilla is found in this account of them instructing Apollos. Although the church met in their home, they still attended meetings in the synagogue. There they heard the gifted preacher, Apollos. It is fascinating to learn that he was a missionary, preaching Christ with "great fervor," yet he didn't even know about the Crucifixion, Resurrection, Ascension, and Pentecost!

Imagine Aquila and Priscilla just waiting for the service to end so they could tell the preacher the rest of the story—the really Good News! Notice that they did not stand up in church and challenge him. "They invited him to their home and explained to him the way of God more adequately" (Acts 18:26).

They could do this because the Holy Spirit was in them. "But when he, the Spirit of truth, comes, he will guide you into all truth" (John 16:13). With the Spirit working in them, Aquila and Priscilla had been taught by Paul. He encouraged those he taught to practice the truths and to teach others to lead. They evidently searched the prophecies with Apollos because when he got to Achaia, he was able to debate the Jews publicly, "proving from the Scriptures that Jesus was the Christ" (Acts 18:28).

8. *Why were all the churches of the Gentiles grateful to Aquila and Priscilla (Rom. 16:4)?* They were honored for their Christian hospitality of course, but in addition to

that, they must have saved Paul's life in some remarkable way. Humanly speaking, if Paul had died, many hundreds of Gentiles would not have heard of salvation in Jesus Christ. Priscilla and Aquila were tools in the hand of God to save Paul for missionary service.

9. *What can you conclude from the fact that their names are always recorded together?* Bob answers, "They were a team, each using his/her talents to serve the Lord. This togetherness suggests that they shared the joy of the work, appreciating each other's talents and contributions."

10. *How does Amos 3:3 comment on their lives together?* This verse reinforces the idea of teamwork—pulling the load evenly and together. It rules out competition between them. We can assume that they experienced great joy and peace and harmony. Priscilla and Aquila were heroes of faith; they shared purpose, direction, and goal. "Now faith is being sure of what we hope for and certain of what we do not see. This is what the ancients were commended for" (Heb. 11:1–2).

11. *Does Priscilla's and Aquila's teaching of Apollos contradict Paul's teaching in 1 Timothy 2:11–12? Explain.* In this day of women's liberation, there has been much discussion of these verses, and there may be many ideas and opinions expressed by group members. To guide the discussion we will point out several facts:
    — Paul's teaching of submission by wives agrees with Peter's teaching in 1 Peter 3:1–2.
    — Teaching is a part of prophesying. The gift of prophecy was given to men and women (Acts 2:16–18; 1 Cor. 12:7–11). This is further evidenced by the mention of several prophetesses: Miriam (Exod. 15:20); Deborah (Judg. 4:4); Huldah (2 Kings

22:14); Isaiah's wife (Isa. 8:3); Anna (Luke 2:36); and the four daughters of Philip (Acts 21:9).

— Priscilla taught *with* her husband.
— Priscilla did not take authority away from her husband or Apollos.
— Priscilla did this teaching in her own home.
— Priscilla and Aquila were Paul's personal pupils and were closely involved with him in his teaching and the practice of it. They would understand the intent of his words. Thus, if this were a violation, they would not be doing it.

12. *Is Priscilla's life an endorsement and encouragement for Christian women to study and teach the Word? See also Luke 10:38–42.* In Priscilla's day, few women were educated. The opposite is true today; most women in Western nations are educated. There is a tremendous interest in Bible study among women in the church today. Bob points out that the Bible does not restrict the teaching role to men. In fact, Proverbs 31:26 says of the ideal woman, "She speaks with wisdom, and faithful instruction is on her tongue."

In the Luke passage, Jesus commended Mary of Bethany for her decision to sit at His feet and learn. We concluded that the Lord wishes to encourage women as well as men to study and teach the Word.

QUESTIONS FOR GROUP DISCUSSION

1. *How could Priscilla and Aquila as a couple be used by the Lord as friends for Paul?* Bob says, "Pastors and preachers are humans. Paul needed a home—an address where he could be reached and a haven of comfort and

security. He needed meals and a place to sleep. He needed hospitality and wanted to be able to exercise hospitality. He needed love. He needed friends who would give him encouragement and advice." Looking again at Paul's words in 1 Corinthians 9:4–6, we detect a note of longing for a home and love. Priscilla and Aquila were used by God to supply this need in Corinth as Lydia was in Philippi (Acts 16:13–15).

(We are reminded of another couple who made a home for one of God's servants, Elisha. See 2 Kings 4:8–11.)

2. *How can a couple serve the Lord by offering hospitality?* Hospitality is generally thought of as room and board, a meal, and/or a place to sleep. Group members may believe, as we do, that there are many more facets to hospitality, such as a warm welcome, a listening ear, an encouraging word, a session of teaching, a prayer of concern. The Lord recognizes this service as done unto Himself.

"Then the righteous will answer him, 'Lord, when did we see you hungry and feed you, or thirsty and give you something to drink? When did we see you a stranger and invite you in, or needing clothes and clothe you? When did we see you sick or in prison and go to visit you?'

"The King will reply, 'I tell you the truth, whatever you did for one of the least of these brothers of mine, you did for me'" (Matt. 25:37–40).

3. *Would this service strengthen or weaken their marriage?* In this lesson we are considering a couple serving the Lord together. Bob and I know from experience that any work we do together for the Lord strengthens our marraige.

4. *Priscilla's name is first in four of the six places they are mentioned (Acts 18:18, 26 [not in KJV]; Rom. 16:3;*

2 Tim. 4:19). Would this indicate that she was the spiritual leader of their home? Explain. Most commentators point out that this order of names (female before male) was unusual, and most conclude that Priscilla was the energetic leader in their home. For instance, D. E. Hiebert says, "The order of their names indicates that Priscilla was the leading spirit in this ministry to Apollos."[1]

On the other hand, Herbert Lockyer states, "If, in any way, Priscilla outshone Aquila, he must have praised God for such a precious, gifted wife."[2]

5. *Do you think she was a domineering woman?* Sexual stereotypes through past centuries have classified strong women who lead as being masculine and domineering. A wife of this type was thought to rob her husband of masculinity.

The verses studied for this lesson cannot be used to support this defunct stereotype. Instead, as Bob says, "Priscilla was a caring, sharing Christian woman." Her aim was not to rule, but to serve the Lord with all her talents. "Domineering" suggests an obnoxious, harsh leadership. If Priscilla had used her abilities in such an abrasive way, she would not have been so lovingly honored by Paul and others.

6. *If the wife is the spiritual leader in a marriage, is she denying her husband's headship (Eph. 5:22–24)?* Since many people struggle with the idea of spiritual leadership in the home, we felt it was appropriate to explore the idea in this lesson. Sometimes only the wife is a Christian. Sometimes the husband refuses to lead or par-

---

[1] D. E. Hiebert, *The Zondervan Pictorial Encyclopedia of the Bible* (Grand Rapids: Zondervan Publishing House, 1975), 1:232.
[2] Herbert Lockyer, *The Women of the Bible* (Grand Rapids: Zondervan Publishing House, 1967), p. 122.

ticipate in the spiritual life of the family. Sometimes the wife may seem more qualified than the husband even though they are both Christians. And sometimes a husband may feel inadequate for the task. What should a woman do in these instances?

We define spiritual leadership as the responsibility to promote spiritual growth, worship, and Christian living in the home.

This passage from Ephesians compares the husband's role in marriage to Christ's role and authority over the church. When this idea of headship is explored (Col. 1:18; Eph. 1:22–23), it is apparent that a husband has the responsibility before God to promote the spiritual growth of the family and to guide them in worship and Christian living. A wife is to be her husband's helper and co-laborer in this task.

If the husband is an unbeliever, the wife bears the responsibility (1 Cor. 7:14), and she will be guided by 1 Peter 3:1–2. If both are Christians and the husband refuses to take his responsibility, the wife should, with due respect, point it out to him as did Sarah to Abraham (Gen. 21:10–12; 1 Peter 3:5–6). This should be done in Christian humility, which in simple language means without a holier-than-thou attitude.

A loving Christian wife will try to understand her husband and encourage him. A loving Christian husband will creatively encourage his wife and other family members to use their talents and abilities for the spiritual growth of all. We agree that having the responsibility does not necessarily mean having superior ability.

Priscilla and Aquila provide a good example for us. If it is true that Priscilla was a talented Christian teacher (assumed from scriptural evidence and the fact that several early churches were named for her, and that Tertullian called her the holy Prisca who preached the gospel), there is no evidence that the use of her talents disrupted the authority structure in their home. Therefore, we conclude that the wife is free to use her talents within that framework of authority.

7. *Would the wife's spiritual leadership weaken or strengthen their marriage or would it not be important? Why?* Discussing this subject further, group members may decide that a wife's spiritual leadership may do any of these three things. In a mixed marriage, a wife's spiritual leadership within the guidelines of Scripture can benefit and strengthen the marriage and family. If a wife belittles an insecure husband who feels inadequate in this area, it can definitely harm or weaken the marriage. If by spiritual leadership we mean the taking af an *active role* in promoting spiritual growth and Christian living, it is unimportant to the marriage who is more active as long as husband and wife work together and are agreed on the matter before the Lord. Bob adds, "Leadership for spiritual growth should be shared by husband and wife for the benefit of both. The husband should try to be the active leader, but if he won't or can't, the wife should help him. This does not necessarily mean that he must be the most fluent and knowledgeable."

8. *Were Aquila and Priscilla leaders in the early church or were they supporters?* From the Bible passsages we have studied in this lesson, we conclude that they were basically supporters and that almost every couple can be used by the Lord as they were. Group members may wish to challenge this conclusion.

9. *Priscilla and Aquila were together in home, business, and church. Would this tend to make their marriage stronger*

or weaker? Explain. Bob answers, "Sometimes 'parting makes the heart grow fonder.' I'm sure they were a typical married couple with problems, frustrations, and irritations that could be magnified by togetherness. But I think they are mentioned in the Bible to show us how useful and strengthening working together for the Lord can be, bonding a couple together in shared lives."

10. *How can Christian couples today be used by the Lord as Aquila and Priscilla were?* Many suggestions may be given: teaching, showing hospitality, etc. Urge the group to be specific—by suggesting ways they can take up this challenge and live it.

The example of Priscilla and Aquila leaves us with little possibility of being excused from service. They served in their everyday life, and so can we.

"Each one should use whatever gift he has received to serve others, faithfully administering God's grace in its various forms. If anyone speaks, he should do it as one speaking the very words of God. If anyone serves, he should do it with the strength God provides, so that in all things God may be praised through Jesus Christ. To him be the glory and power for ever and ever. Amen" (1 Peter 4:10–11).

4

ISAAC AND REBEKAH

BIBLE PASSAGES

Genesis 24; 25:19–28; 26:1–17, 34–35; 27; 28:1–9

OBJECTIVES

1. To point out the importance of marrying a person who is spiritually compatible.
2. To see Isaac and Rebekah as real people.
3. To show that theirs was a loving marriage.
4. To show that Isaac and Rebekah served God and believed in His covenant promise.
5. To examine Isaac's deception of Abimelech and Rebekah's deception of Isaac and to note some far-reaching results.
6. To examine the stress in a marriage when parents have favorite children.
7. To see how God works out His plan through human lives and personalities.
8. To learn if children destroy or contribute to the peace and happiness of marriage.

BACKGROUND

God had called Abraham to leave an idolatrous culture and go to a promised land where he would become the father of many nations. Abraham set out in faith with his wife, Sarah, and their household. God blessed them with material goods, but not with children. After they were physically too old to have children and after God had rejected Ishmael, their "provision of the promised heir," God came to them again and announced the coming birth of Isaac.

This precious miracle child was very close to his parents. He was forty years old and still unmarried when his mother died. Abraham was concerned about his son's loneliness and grief, and he was also concerned that it was time for grand-children to appear on the scene so he could be reassured of God's promise. It was time for Isaac to marry.

QUESTIONS FOR PERSONAL STUDY

1. *Why was it so important that Isaac not marry a Canaanite (Gen. 24:3, 37)?* There were few true believers in Abraham's day. The Canaanites, cursed long before (Gen. 9:25–27), were especially idolatrous. A marriage with one of them would not only corrupt the line of the covenant, but erode the worship of the true God since family ties, influence, and customs were carried into every marriage.

    My husband adds, "It has always been important that God's children 'not be yoked together with unbelievers. For what do righteousness and wickedness have in common? Or what fellowship can light have with darkness?' (2 Cor. 6:14)."

2. *Why was it better for Isaac to marry a relative (Gen. 24:4, 24; 11:26–32; 11:10; 9:26)?* These verses establish the fact that Isaac and Rebekah were relatives and were both direct descendants of Shem, whose God was the Lord (Gen. 9:26). Add to this the fact that Abraham's family was aware of his special call by God. Perhaps the very trauma of separation emphasized the importance of God's call and promise, making a spiritual impact upon the whole family. Therefore, Isaac married a relative who would be sympathetic to and supportive of his worship of God.

3. *Why was Abraham so opposed to Isaac's going to Mesopotamia (Gen. 24:5–7)?* It is safe to assume that Isaac had a submissive, non-assertive nature. This may be seen in the near son-sacrifice incident recorded in Genesis 22 and his passive avoidance of trouble in Gerar (Gen. 26:7, 17–22). Since residence determined possession of the land, Abraham feared that if Isaac met with opposition, he might never return and possess the land which God had promised to Abraham and his heirs.

   In addition to this, Bob feels Abraham had a father's natural reluctance to let a beloved son go. This fear and pain was intensified for Abraham who had waited so long for this promised son.

4. *What can we learn about Rebekah from Genesis 24:16, 18–20, 25, 28, 57–61, 64–65?* She was very beautiful and a virgin. Any girl who could draw enough water for a camel caravan must have had health, strength, and stamina! She was kind and hospitable. She had an open, communicating relationship with her family. She was able to make a difficult decision with strength. She was modest and demonstrated her willingness to recognize Isaac's authority by veiling herself. (I see a tie-in here

with the instructions of Paul in 1 Corinthians 11:2–10, especially verse 10: "For this reason, and because of the angels, the woman ought to have a sign of authority on her head.")

5. *What can we learn about Isaac from Genesis 24:62–67?* Isaac was a quiet, thoughtful man who had been close to his mother. He was tender and loving, and he honored and appreciated his wife.

6. *What does Genesis 25:21–22 tell us about Isaac's and Rebekah's spiritual life?* Isaac prayed for his wife. He knew where to bring his burdens. Rebekah's prayer is the first recorded instance of a woman praying. She, too, turned to the Lord, and He answered her directly. This example of dependence on God and prayer for one another should stimulate all Christian couples to lean on the Lord together.

7. *What does Genesis 26:7 tell us about Isaac as a husband?* We learn that this patriarch was not perfect. He put his own safety before his wife's. He lapsed in faith, in leadership, and in protectiveness for his wife.

8. *Would you do the same? Explain.* Isaac becomes a very real person to us in this passage because most of us put ourselves first. We, too, have times when we are weak in faith and do not trust God to care for us. Even Abraham fell into this sin.

   Bob feels that Isaac was jealous and wanted to stay alive to protect and enjoy his wife and risked her safety as a lesser danger. I wish Isaac had not done this. I would like him much better if he had dared to openly acknowledge and protect his beautiful wife.

9. *What were the results of this lie (Gen. 26:8–11, 26–31)?* Isaac, resting in a false security, forgot himself and openly showed his love for Rebekah. The KJV has, "Isaac

was sporting with Rebekah his wife," and the NIV has, "Abimelech . . . saw Isaac caressing his wife Rebekah." This suggests they were playfully caressing in a way that Abimelech could easily interpret as the comfortable relationship between husband and wife. To Isaac's shame, Abimelech, a pagan, was more worried about sinning than Isaac had been. In protecting himself, Isaac had exposed many others to possible sin and temptation. This certainly did not bring praise to God. God intervened and, ironically, protected and blessed Isaac through Abimelech, and Isaac was given the peace he cherished.

10. *Why did Isaac favor Esau and Rebekah favor Jacob (Gen. 25:27–28)?* This seems to be a case of personalities complementing each other.

11. *What was the birthright blessing which Isaac wanted to give to Esau (Gen. 27:1–4)?* See Genesis 9:26–27; Numbers 7:2; Deuteronomy 21:15–17; 1 Chronicles 5:1–2; 2 Chronicles 21:3. "The birthright was more than a title to the family inheritance; it involved a spiritual position."[1] In looking up these verses, we learn that the birthright was usually given to the eldest son. God was called on to be his God. He became the head of the family, receiving authority and a double portion of the inheritance. The person receiving this blessing carried a weighty load of responsibility as spiritual leader of the family.

12. *Why did Rebekah plot to deceive her husband (Gen. 27:5–17)?* Though Rebekah loved Jacob more than Esau, it seems more likely that she had been so impressed with the prophecy she had received directly from the Lord that she was "helping the Lord to make it come true."

---

[1]W. White, Jr., *Zondervan Pictorial Encyclopedia of the Bible,* (Grand Rapids: Zondervan Publishing House, 1975), 1:617.

13. *Did she know she was doing wrong (Gen. 27:12–13)?*
    Her glib acceptance of any curse which might result
    suggests she was sure she was doing the right thing. In
    her mind, the end justified the means. We, too, often
    "run before the Lord" to save Him embarrassment. What
    presumption on our part! We bend God's law to work
    out His plan. We must learn to "Be still before the Lord
    and wait patiently for him" (Ps. 37:7).

14. *Why were Isaac and Rebekah distressed by Esau's mar-*
    riages (Gen. 26:34–35; 27:46)? Esau married Hittite
    women. The Hittites served many gods, and their social
    structure and customs were dominated by their pagan
    religion. Esau's spiritual life suffered under their
    influence, and their lifestyle was incompatible with that
    of Isaac and Rebekah. Quite likely there were personality
    conflicts too.

15. *When Esau recognized their feelings, how did he try to*
    appease them (Gen. 28:6–9)? Poor Esau! Our hearts are
    touched by his desire to please his parents by marrying
    Ishmael's daughter. He does not put away the evil wives,
    but allies himself with Ishmael, also rejected by God.
    Esau shows that he does not understand or appreciate the
    covenant call and promise given through his father Isaac.

QUESTIONS FOR GROUP DISCUSSION

1. *How did the revelation of Genesis 25:23 affect the lives*
   of Isaac and Rebekah? Isaac was most likely aware of
   God's prophecy to Rebekah. It was as hard for him as it is
   for us to comprehend God's choice. When he recognized Esau's strength, he must have questioned God's
   wisdom or perhaps Rebekah's understanding of the

prophecy. He seems to have favored Esau more to compensate for the hurt and slight Esau would bear.

The obvious conflict between the sons must have made life difficult for the whole family. Rebekah must have often asked, "Why is this happening to me?" (Gen. 25:22). Again and again she thought about the answer she had been given. She was close to Jacob and perhaps directed her best energies to training him to be the head of the family. Ironically, she trained him to lie. Are we ever so misguided?

2. *Is it wrong to favor one child over another?* It is not uncommon for parents to feel closer to or more compatible with one child or another. Sometimes children with handicaps or problems get more attention than the other children in a family. Group members may point out that children need unique, individualized care and concern. Many will agree, however, that to show more favor to one—arbitrarily granting special privileges or tokens of love—is unjust. Bob believes that some favoritism is inevitable and unintentional.

3. *How can favoritism of children cause trouble in a marriage?* When a parent closely identifies with a child and takes his side against the other parent and siblings, hostility is compounded. Children's quarrels that could be easily resolved become family battles. Instead of being one in harmony before the Lord, husband and wife become antagonists, fighting each other and destroying the peace of their home. Deception enters the picture and erodes communication. The marriage is weakened, and everyone loses—especially the children who need strong, unified parental leadership.

4. *Is it ever right to deceive one's mate to attain a good goal? Explain.* Lying is wrong. It builds barriers between hus-

band and wife and introduces a restraint based on guilt and fear of being found out. It erodes the base of trust on which marriage is built and demonstrates an erosion of faith in God's power to make right prevail. Rebekah should have openly reminded Isaac of the prophecy.

Bob points out that we have "lied" to one another to keep a gift or surprise a secret, but this did not involve hurt. He asks, "When deceit causes hurt, can a hurt ever be healed by the 'good goal' which prompted it?"

5. *What do you imagine Isaac's and Rebekah's lives were like after Jacob left (Gen. 26:34–35; 27:42–46; 31:41; 35:27–28)?* Poor Rebekah parted with her dear son thinking it would only be for a short time (Gen. 27:44–45). She never saw him again, and in those days communication with people five hundred miles away was sporadic at best. She never saw her two nieces who married Jacob. She never saw Jacob's children.

Rebekah was left with Esau who probably was angry with her, and his wives who were a grief to her. But she was also left with Isaac, her loving husband. We do not read that he rebuked her for deceiving him. He may have felt God's hand of rebuke on him for trying to circumvent the inheritance prophecy. The Isaac who had taken comfort from Rebekah after his mother's death (Gen. 24:67) could now comfort Rebekah.

We don't know just when Rebekah died. Isaac, who was considered old and near death at the time of Jacob's departure, surprised everyone and lived to be 180, having the longest life of any of the patriarchs. He was alive when Jacob returned more than twenty years later. Some scholars believe Isaac died about the time Joseph, his grandson, became a ruler in Egypt. Jacob and Esau buried their father.

6. *Who was more likable, Jacob or Esau?* Answers may vary here, but many people will agree that it is easier to like Esau.

   Esau fits the sex-stereotype of the vigorous male. We keenly feel his anger and disappointment when he does not receive the birthright blessing. We are touched when he tries to right his wrongs and please his parents by marrying one of Ishmael's daughters. He is lovable when he meets Jacob and his family. He runs to Jacob, embraces him, weeps with him, meets his family, refuses Jacob's gift, and offers to have his men protect Jacob (Gen. 33:4–17).

   In contrast, Jacob impresses us as being manipulative and manipulated in the birthright matter. We quiver with righteous indignation when we read of Jacob's lies to his father, even saying that God was helping him. And then he betrayed his brother with a kiss (Gen. 27:26–27)! Jacob seems fearful and weak in some events in his life, but he also demonstrated persistence and a willingness to work hard and long for the people and things he valued. Most important, he feared God.

7. *Why did God choose Jacob to receive the promise?* We may wonder, but we may not question God's sovereign right to choose whomever He wishes. The Bible does help us understand, though. We are told that Esau despised his birthright (Gen. 25:34), while Jacob wanted it so badly that he lied to get it. When Samuel wondered about God's choice of a king to replace Saul, he was told by the Lord, "The Lord does not look at the things man looks at. Man looks at the outward appearance, but the Lord looks at the heart" (1 Sam. 16:7). First Corinthians 1:26–31 is even more helpful: "But God chose the foolish things of the world to shame the wise; God chose

the weak things of the world to shame the strong. . . . so that no one may boast before him" (vv. 27, 29). God is to receive the glory, not man. Jacob discovered over and over the folly of leaning on one's own understanding. He fled to God time and again for intervention and protection in the difficulties of life (Gen. 28:16–17, 20–22; 31:28–29; 32:7–12; 35:3). By studying Jacob's life, we can see that man cannot save himself. God receives the glory and honor which are His alone.

8. *Do children contribute to the peace and happiness of marriage or do they destroy it? Explain.* As children grow, they cause their parents to grow spiritually, emotionally, and intellectually. Growth involves energy, some pain, great delight, and change. Couples who choose not to have children because they will bring challenge and conflict into a marriage are limiting the scope of God's power, the size of the canvas on which He creates beauty. With God's blessing, the challenges of parenting develop personal qualities such as understanding, patience, self-control, and humor. These enrich the marriage relationship. Parenting widens a couple's world, giving them new and ever-changing interests. It directs them away from soul-shrinking self-centeredness.

Bob comments, "In a truly Christian home, peace is experienced even when difficulties are encountered." We agree that the love and peace and happiness that grow when we share joy and suffering as parents are beyond anything we dreamed of.

9. *What advice might Isaac and Rebekah give to couples today?* Bob suggests that Isaac and Rebekah would tell us these four things:

— Trust in the Lord and do not "run before Him."
— Show love to all your children—as evenly as possible.

— Do not deceive each other.

— Communicate with each other or problems will result.

Isaac and Rebekah wanted children. They made many mistakes and had many heartaches. Somehow I believe they would agree with the author of Proverbs when he says:

> Let love and faithfulness never leave you;
>   bind them around your neck,
>   write them on the tablet of your heart.
> Then you will win favor and a good name
>   in the sight of God and man.
> Trust in the Lord with all your heart
>   and lean not on your own understanding;
> in all your ways acknowledge him,
>   and he will make your paths straight.
> Do not be wise in your own eyes;
>   fear the Lord and shun evil.
> This will bring health to your body
>   and nourishment to your bones (Prov. 3:3–8).

5

ANANIAS AND SAPPHIRA

BIBLE PASSAGE

Acts 4:32–5:12

OBJECTIVES

1. To explore the reasons why Ananias and Sapphira agreed to give a partial gift and lie about it.
2. To discuss God's judgment on them for their sin.
3. To explore the advantages and disadvantages of Christian communal life.
4. To notice some of the pitfalls in Christian giving.
5. To examine and evaluate our commitment as stewards of God's wealth.

BACKGROUND

The risen Christ had commanded His followers to wait in Jerusalem for the gift of the Holy Spirit (Acts 1:4–5). Bewildered by His ascension into heaven, but ready to serve joyfully, they obediently returned to Jerusalem and devoted themselves to prayer and worship (Acts 1:12–14; Luke 24:52).

Peter became the spokesman and leader of this small nucleus of believers. He anticipated the church's need for leaders in the task of evangelizing the world, and he suggested they elect an apostle to take the place of Judas. Matthias was chosen to be the twelfth apostle.

When the Holy Spirit was poured into the believers on Pentecost, Peter spoke to the crowds of curious Jews and proclaimed the resurrection and kingship of Jesus Christ. About three thousand people responded to Peter's call to repent and be baptized.

These new believers clung together in joy, fear, and wonder. They were so filled with love that they shared all they owned. Their lives were united into one continuous worship festival. And the Lord added to their number each day.

QUESTIONS FOR PERSONAL STUDY

1. *Why did the new believers adopt this communal lifestyle (Acts 2:44; 4:32)?* They were one in heart and mind. The love of God overwhelmed them and enabled them to put selfish ambitions aside and to share everything with the other believers.
2. *Did everyone receive an equal amount of the communal goods (Acts 2:45; 4:35)?* Atheistic communist political systems seek to equalize the distribution of goods and possessions. Christian communism recognizes the vast variety of people and circumstances created by God and ministers to each person according to his or her need.
3. *What was the result of this sharing (Acts 4:34)?* There was

not a needy person among them. Not one new Christian was consumed by anxiety or coveting. Their energies were translated into loving provision for one another.

4. *What was the significance of laying the gifts at the apostles' feet (Acts 4:35, 37; 5:2)?* The apostles, as God's representatives, received these gifts in His name and assumed the responsibility for their distribution much as the priests in Old Testament times received and distributed the tithes of God's people.

5. *Why did Ananias and Sapphira sell their property?* After reading Acts 4:32–37, I get the feeling that the new Christians in their loving enthusiasm assumed that all of their fellow believers would join them in selling and sharing their possessions. Sin entered the situation and social pressure—instead of spiritual spontaneity— motivated them to give. Bob states it simply, "Ananias and Sapphira didn't want people to talk about them because they hadn't sold their property and given the money to the apostles."

6. *Why did they hold some money back?* Bob says, "They were not sincere in their commitment to Christ. They wanted to serve 'God and Money'" (Matt. 6:24). Perhaps somewhere in their minds they harbored a fear for the future: What if this movement collapsed? What if there were no more to share? Just in case this happened, they would hold a little back—put it away "for a rainy day." As Peter pointed out (Acts 5:4), they were free to do whatever they liked with the money.

By holding a portion back, they indicated they were not totally committed to the Lord. Perhaps they were "trial Christians." The Lord calls us to total commitment.

7. *Why did they say they were giving all the money (Acts 5:3)?* This was their sin. They wanted to "look as good as

the others." They wanted praise for their piety. They were more interested in the approbation of men than of God.

This passage ties in well with James 1 and 2. Ananias and Sapphira are examples of the double-minded person (James 1:7–8; 4:8–10) who foolishly honors social status (James 2:1–7). They tried to cover their faltering faith with a show of good works.

8. *Why did Peter say they had lied to the Holy Spirit (Acts 5:3–4, 9)?* The only One who knew they were lying was the Holy Spirit. They blatantly tried to convince the Holy Spirit in Peter that they were telling the truth.

When Peter speaks of lying to the Holy Spirit, he asserts that the Holy Spirit is truly a Person and not just a force or influence.

9. *Why did God strike them dead? See Deuteronomy 23:21–23; Romans 11:22.* By insisting that they were giving all the money, they in essence vowed or dedicated all the money to God. Thus, when they held some back, they cheated God. The Deuteronomy passage demonstrates God's attitude toward such an action.

This was also a major attack by Satan on the new church. God chose to punish this sin in a dramatic way to impress on them God's hatred of hypocrisy (Matt. 23:25–36).

10. *Because Ananias and Sapphira were struck dead (Acts 5:5, 10), do you believe they never were truly saved and committed to the Lord?* Bob answers, "The church is full of sinning Christians who believe in the forgiveness of sins. God may pronounce judgment on sin in any way He chooses. Ananias and Sapphira must have declared their faith in Christ and may have been saved, but God used their deaths to warn His people of the sins of hypocrisy and love of money (1 Tim. 6:10).

If this question is discussed by the group, members may wish to read and consider Matthew 7:21–23 and Jude 22–23.

11. *How did the judgment on them affect the church (Acts 5:5, 11)?* Naturally, the people were afraid. They must have examined their own hearts and lives. As Bob says, "This put the fear of God in them." They were reminded of His holiness and His hatred of sin.

QUESTIONS FOR GROUP DISCUSSION

1. *Compare the Christian communism of the early church with Marxist communism today.* Marxist communism is godless. Christian communism is God-centered. Practical aspects of the systems illustrate this great difference in philosophy: Marxist communism is cruel and unjust in many ways; all the people in a given country are forced to be a part of the system. Christian communism stresses love, mercy, and justice, and people are free to join or leave the system.

2. *Does Christian communal living as it is practiced by some today strengthen marriages?* Some have suggested that the support of the whole group encourages and strengthens each member, thereby freeing marriage partners from some anxieties that could weaken their marriage. Others have cited a lack of privacy and stronger allegiance to the group than the nuclear family as factors that weaken a marriage.

3. *Is a Christian communal lifestyle desirable for large groups or groups from mixed cultures (Acts 6:1)?* The little church grew from 120 members (Acts 1:15) to 3,000 (Acts 2:41) and then to more than 5,000 (Acts 4:4)

in a matter of days. It wasn't long before the administration of such a system became difficult and eventually impractical. It also fostered discrimination based on cultural loyalties. This leads us to believe that the communal system is best when adopted by small groups who can be particularly helped by that lifestyle. Most Christians can experience the unity and fellowship of believers in the congregational setting.

4. *What does it say about their marriage that Ananias and Sapphira agreed to withhold part of the money?* We can infer that they discussed such matters and were a close and communicating couple. They must have had the same values and goals. They were more loyal to each other than to God.

5. *In marriage, two become one. What does this lesson say about the individual accountability of each marriage partner to God? Was Sapphira too loyal?* Acts 5:1–6 clearly shows that whether married or not, we are individually accountable to God. Yes, Sapphira was too loyal to her husband. She should have confessed and sought forgiveness. This would have demonstrated her loyalty to God.

6. *If everyone in our churches today who committed the same sins as Ananias and Sapphira (i.e., not keeping their vows to God, lying for personal recognition, or giving dimes when they could give dollars) were cast out of the church, do you think membership rolls would shrink much? Explain.* Most, if not all, of us struggle with sinful self as Paul did (Rom. 7:15–19). James also laments, "We all stumble in many ways. If anyone is never at fault in what he says, he is a perfect man, able to keep his whole body in check" (James 3:2).

If the drastic action suggested in this question were effected, our churches would probably be empty, with not even a pastor to give a call to worship. We see, then, that the account of Ananias and Sapphira is included in the Bible to "put the fear of God in *us*" so that we will examine our hearts and lives and ask, "Am I truly committed to the Lord? Is this reflected in my words and deeds?"

7. *If publicly laying the gifts at the apostles' feet fostered competition for recognition, may we conclude that all giving should be done anonymously? See Matthew 6:1–4.* The Matthew passage rules out personal recognition or praise as a *motive* for giving. However, the act of giving has always been a part of worship, beginning with the offerings brought by Cain and Abel (Gen. 4:3–5). There is certainly an honorable place for anonymous giving, but many times "the gift without the giver is bare."

I can illustrate this from my own life. Trying to practice the teaching of Matthew 6:1–4, I once sent a Christmas plant to a young woman who is a member of our church. I enclosed an unsigned note saying that the gift was an expression of Christian love and appreciation for her cheerful Christian spirit.

The next time I saw her, she seemed sad and troubled. She told me about the anonymous gift and said that her husband (not a believer) was sure she had a lover in the church. Their marriage was floundering because of my well-intentioned gift! I explained immediately, and she said, "It would have been so much nicer if you had signed your name. Then I would have felt your love and thought about it whenever I saw you."

8. *What should a couple do if they disagree on the amount to be given or the causes to be given to?* Here we can learn something positive from Ananias and Sapphira. They communicated with each other on this subject— talked it out and reached an agreement.

Bob suggests several things to consider:
— Are both committed Christians?
— Are both practical and responsible in spending so that giving to the Lord does not suffer?
— Do both husband and wife understand each other's reasons and wishes in this matter?
— If there is one wage earner, do both still have a voice in the spending of the money?
— Does each partner tithe his/her separate income?
— Do they combine their funds and then tithe?

We have struggled with this matter in our own marriage and have found that communication—talking it out lovingly and understanding each other's backgrounds, reasons, and attitudes—is the answer to this problem. This communication is an ongoing process.

9. *How can giving be made equally joyful and satisfying for each marriage partner?* This question arises because we have been frustrated with the lack of meaning in our church offerings for general expenses. The one who holds the checkbook or manages the money has some sense of an active role, but the other does not. Often the offertory prayer is meaningless ritual. To combat this, we have discussed and recognized the fact that this regular weekly offering is a necessity and we set aside the money for this offering as soon as the paycheck is cashed. When asked for large gifts for other causes, we talk it over, taking into account the need, the stewardship of those who handle the funds, our resources, and then we ask if God has somehow laid this need upon our hearts. It is necessary to do this because we—as do most people— receive hundreds of mail requests for money each year.

When deciding how much to give or pledge, we sometimes each write the amount we are considering on a piece of paper and exchange papers. Often we have chosen the same amount or can easily compromise.

In addition to this, we allow each other freedom to give spontaneously, expressing our own personalities. For example, I like to send flowers to people to express appreciation or encouragement. Bob likes to give gifts of food to help someone struggling with a low income. We both give small anonymous gifts of money occasionally. We trust each other to be wise.

Whenever we have given beyond what we thought we could afford, the Lord has amply supplied our needs. We have experienced the truth and joy of Malachi 3:10: "'Bring the whole tithe into the storehouse, that there may be food in my house. Test me in this,' says the Lord Almighty, 'and see if I will not throw open the floodgates of heaven and pour out so much blessing that you will not have room enough for it.'"

10. *Does this lesson suggest any ways in which you or your church could make giving more meaningful or more effective?* We suggest the following which may start discussion:

— Encourage the pastor to preach from God's Word on the need and desire to give joyfully.

— Try the "faith-promise" method for giving time and money. In this method, believers prayerfully decide what they can give on a monthly basis for the coming year and then pledge this anonymously. Their pledge is based on their faith that God will enable them to keep this promise.

— Do not recognize the size or amount of one believer's gift over another by placing the names of those who give large amounts on a plaque, a church window, or similar types of recognition.

This discussion of giving is not complete without the teaching of Jesus in Luke 21:1–4 to give us proper perspective. "As he looked up, Jesus saw the rich putting their gifts into the temple treasury. He also saw a poor widow put in two very small copper coins. 'I tell you the truth,' he said, 'this poor widow has put in more than all the others. All these people gave their gifts out of their wealth; but she out of her poverty put in all she had to live on.' "

With commitment like hers, we will not be likely to fall into the sin of Ananias and Sapphira.

6

JACOB, LEAH, AND RACHEL

BIBLE PASSAGES

Genesis 29–33; 35:16–29

OBJECTIVES

1. To study Laban's deception and the problems and grief it caused.
2. To trace the spiritual growth of Rachel and Leah.
3. To analyze the stresses caused by multiple marriage and domination of in-laws.
4. To consider how children may be affected by a parent's second marriage.
5. To see how God worked out His plan through these tragic circumstances.

BACKGROUND

In the chapters just before our lesson passages, there is the account of Jacob and his mother, Rebekah, scheming to deceive his father, Isaac, into giving him the birthright blessing instead of his brother, Esau. When Esau heard of this, he was so angry that he planned to kill Jacob immediately after their father died.

Rebekah wanted to get her favorite son, Jacob, out of danger, but she did not want Isaac to know about Esau's threat. So she decided it was time for Jacob to marry and that he should not take a wife from the local people as Esau had done, bringing them heartache (Gen. 27:46). She suggested to Isaac that Jacob go to her family, who lived about 450 miles to the northeast, to choose a wife. Isaac readily agreed to the plan because his father had sent a servant to the same family to find him a wife—Rebekah. Isaac again pronounced the covenant promise and blessing to Jacob and sent him on his way.

Jacob, the homebody, beloved of his mother, had to say good-by to her forever and set out on a long, difficult journey. He had to pay for his deceit with long years of exile.

QUESTIONS FOR PERSONAL STUDY

1. *Why did Jacob go to Paddan Aram? See Genesis 27:41– 28:5.* Jacob went to Paddan Aram for two reasons: to escape from his brother Esau who planned to kill him as soon as their father died, and to marry one of his Uncle Laban's daughters.

2. *Explain Jacob's actions in Genesis 29:10–12.* Jacob was so overcome by relief and emotion when he learned that he had reached his destination and that the shepherdess before him was his cousin, that he received special strength to move the heavy stone from the mouth of the well. His emotion had to be translated into action. He

wept with joy and relief and kissed Rachel because he was so glad to be with family again, so glad he had reached a home where he belonged. I am sure he fell in love with Rachel right then.

3. *What does Genesis 29:17 mean when it says Leah had "weak eyes" or "tender eyes" (KJV)? How would this affect her appearance?* For years people have read "tender eyed" in the King James Version and some have assumed this meant that Leah was very gentle and had a "sweet look." Later translations more correctly indicate that her eyes were weak or delicate. Some commentators suggest that she had an eye disease common to desert dwellers; constant exposure to wind and sand caused their eyes to become red and painful. Some think she was nearsighted and squinted all the time. Either could have been true and would have distorted her face enough to obscure any loveliness she might have had. Compared with Rachel's fresh, young beauty, the older Leah, with red, strained eyes, was undesirable. Laban probably knew it was unlikely that anyone would choose her for a wife.

4. *How much did Jacob love Rachel (Gen. 29:20)?* Seven years of hard labor is a high price to pay for any bride, but they seemed like a few days to Jacob because he loved Rachel so much. The irony and the agony of this story is that Jacob actually worked fourteen years for Rachel. He was given Leah for the first seven years' work (even though he did not agree to work for her as his bride), and then he was asked to pledge to work another seven years for Rachel. He didn't hesitate to do so.

5. *What do you suppose motivated Laban to deceive Jacob (Gen. 29:23–27)?* Laban's deceit was despicable. He justified it by citing a tradition that a younger daughter

should not be married before an older daughter. We discount this motive and see only that he recognized the value of Jacob's "free" labor and the blessings he received because of Jacob. He wanted to benefit as long as possible.

6. *Why didn't Jacob realize he had been deceived (Gen. 29:25)?* This question requires some speculation, but every group with which I have studied this material has wanted to spend a little time wondering how this could have happened. Bob thinks brides must have been heavily veiled until after the marriage was consummated. Some people have suggested that Leah planned the deceit with her father and so did not speak and betray her identity. Others defend her and say her father probably threatened her. I agree with those who remind us that wedding feasts in Bible times involved drinking; thus, Jacob may have been slightly drunk and not too observant.

Whatever the reason, Jacob *was* deceived. It does not take much imagination to speculate about Leah's fear at being discovered, Rachel's anger and bitterness at being confined and not allowed to go to her own wedding, and Jacob's sick heart as he felt the trap sprung on him.

7. *What law did God later give to avoid family tragedies such as this one? See Leviticus 18:18.* This verse reads, "Do not take your wife's sister as a rival wife and have sexual relations with her while your wife is living." If this law had been in effect in Jacob's time, he would not have been able to marry Rachel. Today, however, a fraudulent marriage such as that between Jacob and Leah would be annulled, but the scars from the trauma would still be there and any sisterly love would probably be destroyed.

8. *What was Leah's greatest trial (Gen. 29:31)?* Leah's greatest trial was not being loved by her husband. This is

clear from the names she gave her sons. She had sexual relations with Jacob occasionally, but the Bible does not equate that with love.

9. *What was Rachel's greatest trial (Gen. 30:1)?* Rachel had the devoted love of her husband, but she had no children. In those days a wife fulfilled her part of the marriage contract by having children. If she did not, she was despised and had no social status. Rachel's sterility was such a trial to her that it made her lash out and blame her husband.

10. *What was Jacob's greatest trial in his marriage (Gen. 29:25; 30:1, 16, 29–30; 31:1–2, 31, 38–42; 32:6–8; 35:16–20; 49:31)?* Jacob had many trials in his marriage, and most of them seem to have been caused by his father-in-law who deceived him and was his demanding employer. I can imagine Jacob's grief for Rachel in her barrenness. It reminds me of Elkanah, Hannah, and Peninnah (1 Sam. 1:1–8). When Hannah grieved because she was childless while Peninnah had children, Elkanah tried to comfort her by saying, "Don't I mean more to you than ten sons?" I can imagine Jacob saying something similar to Rachel.

He was an object of barter between his wives. He worried about providing for his household. His brothers-in-law were jealous of him. He was afraid of his father-in-law's power over him. He was always working to the point of exhaustion. He feared that his own brother would kill him and his family. His beloved wife, Rachel, died at an early age. Leah, too, died before he did.

11. *What does the incident recorded in Genesis 30:15 tell us about the relationship between Rachel and Leah?* This account gives us a glimpse of the bitter competition and

jealousy between the sisters. Each felt that Jacob should be exclusively hers—Leah because she married him first, and Rachel because he loved her. It seems that Jacob lived with Rachel and only visited Leah.

A word must be added here about mandrakes. They were small fruits that grew in a rosette of leaves. They were regarded as an aphrodisiac—a love potion to make one desirable and fertile. At this point in her life, Rachel was still looking for a human answer to her barrenness.

12. *What spiritual growth or progress can you see in Leah's naming of her children (Gen. 29:32–35; 30:11–12, 18, 20)?* Judging from the names she gave her children, it seems Leah was a true child of God who turned to Him in confidence that He would see her misery and help her. After having three sons, she was less obsessed with her lovelorn state, so when Judah was born she reached a spiritual peak, praising the Lord. She regarded her own children and her "step" children as sources of joy, precious gifts from the Lord, but she was still haunted by the desire to be honored by her husband.

13. *What spiritual growth or progress can you see in Rachel's naming of her children (Gen. 30:6, 8, 24; 35:18)?* When Rachel blamed Jacob for her lack of children, he answered, "Am I in the place of God, who has kept you from having children?" (Gen. 30:2). She must then have pleaded with God because she saw Dan's birth as an answer to prayer. But when Naphtali was born, she was again focusing on her competition with Leah. She again recognized God in Joseph's birth. When her second son was born and she lay dying, she was caught up in her agony and named him "Ben-Oni," "Son of my trouble."

14. *Why do you suppose God gave Leah all her children before giving Rachel even one of her own?* When we

compare Leah and Rachel, Leah seems to have been the true believer—more beautiful spiritually. Yet when we realize how close Rachel was to her son Joseph and read of his beautiful faith and life (Gen. 39:9; 40:8; 41:16, 51–52; 42:18; 45:5, 8), we may conclude that she trained him well and perhaps grew spiritually in the tragedies and trials she experienced. We believe God had to teach Rachel His power and develop her commitment and patience before she was ready for her great task—mothering and training Joseph whom God had called to deliver His people from famine.

15. *What do we learn about this marriage from Genesis 31:4–7, 14–18?* It seems that the years mellowed the three and they learned to work and decide things together as a family unit.

16. *Do you suppose that the different value placed by Jacob on his wives and children (Gen. 33:1–2) had anything to do with the rivalries between his children and the tribes that descended from them?* This different value is also brought out in Genesis 37:3–4 which tells of the brothers' resentment of the favorite son, Joseph. It caused trouble and competition among the brothers. The tribes descending from Dan, Naphtali, Gad, and Asher, who were the sons born to the servant girls, were less prominent and less devout.

17. *Both Rachel and Leah gave birth to a deliverer of God's people (Gen. 30:24; 45:5–8; 29:35; Matt. 1:2–16). Who were they?* Rachel was the mother of Joseph who delivered God's people from famine. Leah was the mother of Judah whose descendants were the kings of the line of David; ultimately she was honored by becoming the "mother" of Jesus who came to save His people from their sins as God had promised.

QUESTIONS FOR GROUP DISCUSSION

1. *What effect did these two marriages in one week have on Jacob's and Rachel's love?* Their shining love, which had grown through the years, was tarnished and corroded in one night. Jacob must have been angry and frustrated. He had planned to devote all his love and energy to caring for Rachel. He must have cheered many difficult hours during those seven years with the thought that soon she would be his very own wife. Rachel, loved so dearly, must have felt privileged and chosen. She looked forward to intimacy with Jacob and being cherished by him the rest of her life. Now that intimacy which they had dreamed of belonged to another, and Rachel fell from first choice to second place. Bob observes that they received a mental and emotional blow from which they never fully recovered. Their wedding night must have been spent in tears.

2. *With whom are your sympathies in this marriage triangle?* It surprised me that Bob's sympathies were with Rachel and Leah because my first sympathy was for Jacob. Bob pointed out that the sisters probably had no choice in the matter. They were used by their father for his ends. Any love they may have thought he had for them, his daughters, was lost, and their sisterly love was destroyed. It was a true bereavement.

   I felt sorry for the lonely Jacob who had already lost his home with his parents, Isaac and Rebekah, because of deception. I could imagine him out on the hills in a bitter cold rain, caring for the sheep and dreaming of the time when Rachel would warm his heart and body. I could feel his hurt at being betrayed and sense his sudden understanding of Esau's hurt years before. So guilt was added to his burden of grief, disappointment, and confusion. How he must have cried to God for mercy and justice.

In discussing why we felt as we did, we found a reflection of how we care for each other, how we respond to each other's helplessness and need. It was a beautiful realization, and we thank God for the love He has given us.

3. *How important is beauty in the selection of a marriage partner?* As Christians, we remember that God looks at the heart. And, as we read in Proverbs 31:30, "Charm is deceptive, and beauty is fleeting; but a woman who fears the Lord is to be praised."

We must add, though, that a man looking for a wife is definitely attracted by beauty, and he appreciates it. And a woman wants to be beautiful for her husband (Prov. 31:22–23). But, as Bob says, there is no guarantee that physical beauty will last—a beautiful girl may become unkempt or be disfigured by disease or accident—so a wise man will not place much importance on outer beauty. He will look for lasting inner beauty—spiritual commitment to serve the Savior, love, loyalty, understanding, unselfishness, sensitivity to people's needs, and all those qualities listed in Proverbs 31:10–31, which describes a wife of noble character.

As it happened, Rachel, the beauty, died in her youth, and Leah was the wife who grew old with Jacob. She lived with him through his suffering during Joseph's absence and was a comfort to him because she had learned to look to God for comfort in times of anguish.

4. *Was Jacob happy?* Jacob had many problems and days of anguish, but we believe that in general he was happy. He seemed to enjoy his work and his children. He was

blessed with material goods. He and his wives seemed to adjust to their plural marriage (which was not uncommon in those days). In all of these outward and earthly things Jacob seemed to enjoy a measure of happiness.

Far more important, though, was the spiritual joy Jacob was given in all his trials. God Himself spoke with Jacob on his lonely flight from home and gave him a wonderful promise, to which Jacob responded with a vow (Gen. 28:10–22). He was conscious of the Lord's hand of blessing on him and the people he lived with (Gen. 30:30; 31:4–9). He communicated freely with God (Gen. 31:11–16). He wrestled with God and obtained a special blessing (Gen. 32:22–32). After the Shechem massacre, he realized his family had backslidden, and he came back to sweet fellowship with God (Gen. 34; 35:1–15). He experienced God's patience and forgiveness and learned the joy of dependence on our faithful God.

5. *How does the Lord regard polygamy?* The Lord teaches that marriage is the union of two people, male and female. This is the ideal. Monogamy is what God wants for His people. Yet He tolerated polygamy—especially, it seems, in days when many men were killed in hand-to-hand combat. In fact, His law, which provided that a man cohabit with the childless widow of his brother so that she could keep her place in society and keep his inheritance intact, seemed designed to remedy this problem caused by a shortage of men (Gen. 38:8–11; Deut. 25:5–6).

Yet it must be pointed out that all the polygamous marriages told about in the Bible were beset with problems, and Jesus renewed the concept and ideal of monogamous marriage in very strong terms (Matt. 19:3–12).

6. *Are the multiple marriages of today anything like the polygamous marriages recorded in the Bible?* Bob answers, "Men don't live under the same roof with multiple wives today, but the problems of having had more than one wife—complications of loyalty, rivalry, discipline and training of children, economic and spiritual considerations—are similar to those encountered in polygamous homes." Perhaps this is why one of the qualifications for church leaders is "husband of one wife" (1 Tim. 3:2, 12).

7. *Jacob worked for his father-in-law. What problems did he encounter? Do some couples face similar problems today?* Ann Landers, the well-known advice columnist, gets many letters on this problem. Jacob felt obligated to please his father-in-law to an extent not required of a financially independent son-in-law. Constant close association in business and private life encourages irritability and interference in private affairs.

8. *If in-laws control or dominate a marriage, what should be done? What did Jacob do?* Jacob recognized separation as the answer, and that still seems to be the practical solution in most cases.

9. *In homes where a parent has been married more than once is there a tendency to show more love to the children of the best-loved mate?* A conscientious parent will love each child as an individual. But likeness to a beloved mate, especially if that mate has died and the parent is less happy in a second marriage, will evoke nostalgia and may cause the parent to give special attention to that child(ren). This, of course, complicates matters.

10. *The marriage blessing given to Ruth and Boaz (Ruth 4:11) states: "May the Lord make the woman who is*

coming into your home like Rachel and Leah. . . ."
Would you welcome such a blessing on your marriage?
This is a trick question written in a way that should pro-
voke discussion. The Bible does not say, "May your wife
have a personality like Leah's and Rachel's all rolled into
one." No, the rest of the sentence must be read: "like
Rachel and Leah, who together built up the house of
Israel." This was a wish that Boaz and Ruth might have
children and work together for the building of God's
kingdom.

11. *Why did God include in the Bible this account of a trian-*
gular marriage with its problems and jealousies? God
uses this to warn us of the problems that come with
multiple marriage.

More important, though, is the revelation of the love,
mercy, and forgiveness of our gracious God who "re-
deems our messes." We struggle through life with our
sinful natures and become despondent and frustrated
when we fail or our plans are foiled; yet even in those
circumstances God is working out His wonderful plan
through us—and often in spite of us. We may bring our
cares and problems to Him, knowing that "in all things
God works for the good of those who love him, who have
been called according to his purpose" (Rom. 8:28).

7

AMRAM AND JOCHEBED

BIBLE PASSAGES

Exodus 1; 2:1–10; 6:18–20; Numbers 26:59–60; Hebrews 11:23–27

OBJECTIVES

1. To understand the tension in their lives.
2. To compare Pharaoh's reasoning to ideas on abortion today.
3. To learn why Amram and Jochebed were unafraid to do what was right.
4. To see God's purpose and guiding hand in saving Moses.
5. To recognize children as gifts from God.
6. To understand the importance of early childhood training.

BACKGROUND

When Jacob and his family packed up and moved to Egypt, they were given the best part of the land and were kept separate from the Egyptians (Gen. 46:31–47:12). They were protected by the government because they were Joseph's relatives and he was the ruler of Egypt. "The Israelites settled in Egypt in the region of Goshen. They acquired property there and were fruitful and increased greatly in number" (Gen. 47:27).

The key to this lesson is found in Exodus 1:8: "Then a new king, who did not know about Joseph, came to power in Egypt." This king felt no obligation to care for these foreigners. Instead, he felt threatened by their growing strength and began persecuting them so they would fear and obey him. It was in these circumstances that Amram and Jochebed married and brought their children into the world.

QUESTIONS FOR PERSONAL STUDY

1. *Why were Amram and Jochebed not named in Exodus 1 and 2?* It seems that our attention is to be directed to the saving of Moses. His parents, his sister, and Pharaoh's daughter were all instruments used by the Lord for that end. This was the most significant event in the lives of Amram and Jochebed. This coupled with the fact that all three of their children became leaders of God's people provides good reason for us to study them as a couple and as parents living in time of persecution.

2. *Why didn't Pharaoh want the Hebrews to leave his country (Exod. 1:10–11)?* The Hebrews were originally a separate group of shepherds living in Goshen. As they multiplied, more jobs were needed, and they became a significant segment of the Egyptian work force. Pharaoh could not have accomplished his ambitious building projects without the Hebrew laborers.

3. *Why did the Hebrews multiply even more under oppres-*

sion (Exod. 1:12)? God is always in control and would not let Pharaoh succeed in crushing His people. Instead, He made them more numerous and powerful. It may also be suggested that this persecution drew couples closer and more children resulted from this strengthened intimacy.

4. *The Hebrews' lives were made bitter (Exod. 1:14). What effect would Amram's long working hours doing work he hated and being mistreated have had on his marriage relationship?* During this time of persecution, the Hebrew men were seldom home. Many died or were seriously injured. They were exhausted and angry at injustice. At home, the women had to do their own work and the men's work. Their lives were in jeopardy. Husbands and wives could not fully share in the training of their children. They could not plan and dream together. In fact, unless they were trusting God to deliver them, they had no hope of pleasure or joy from day to day. This would tend to encourage self-pity or a negative attitude of hoplessness—a living for the present with no hope of a future. Marriage under these circumstances may be contrasted with the marriage of Abraham and Sarah which, though tested, was strengthened by trust in God and glowing hope for the future.

5. *The midwives were ordered to kill the Hebrew boy babies before they drew a breath (Exod. 1:16). If they were not there soon enough, the babies were allowed to live (Exod. 1:18–19). What do you suppose was the reasoning behind this?* As I understand this, Pharaoh was clinging to some justification for his plan to control Hebrew population growth. If he could reason that a child was not a true person until it drew a breath and so "became alive," he could not be accused of murdering the Hebrew children—because legally they had not yet

lived. In this way he hoped to justify his action and avoid a revolt. Of course, the mothers knew that their children were living human beings since conception. They had felt that prenatal life! They wanted their children to live so they didn't call the midwives soon enough; and the midwives didn't hurry to get to them. There is truth in the midwives' excuse to Pharaoh, though. Statistics prove that women who are active physically, working hard as these Hebrew women did, are more likely to have a shorter, easier labor than inactive women.

6. *How did God reward the midwives (Exod. 1:21)?* God rewarded these midwives with children of their own. The implications of this will be discussed in question 4 of the "Questions for Group Discussion."

7. *Note the age difference between Moses and Aaron (Exod. 7:7). How would this have made it more difficult for Amram and Jochebed to hide Moses?* Bob says, "That little three-year-old tongue might tell family secrets—just as little tongues do today."

8. *Why were Moses' parents not afraid of the king's edict (Heb. 11:23)?* They knew they were doing right and that God was on their side. They had faith in God's triumph over sin. They knew their child was "special."

9. *How did this bear fruit in their son's life (Heb. 11:27)?* Moses, too, was given the gift of faith. He had been taught what was right and that great blessing comes to the righteous. God's blessing on his parents' courageous plan to save him and train him encouraged him to choose to suffer with the people of God, believing in their ultimate victory and happiness, rather than enjoy political security and cultural advantage for a short time.

10. *Jochebed planned a most creative way to save Moses. What promise were she and Amram trusting God to keep*

(Gen. 3:15; 28:14; 1 John 3:8)? Ever since Adam and Eve had fallen into sin and God had given the promise of a child born of a woman who would crush the Devil, women had hoped and prayed that their child would be this Promised One. Jochebed believed God could work deliverance through her child. This made her bold and creative in her plan to save Moses.

QUESTIONS FOR GROUP DISCUSSION

1. *Compare Exodus 2:2, Acts 7:20, and Hebrews 11:23. It seems that Amram and Jochebed decided to save Moses because he was "no ordinary" child. Does this imply that we are not called upon to use extraordinary means to save every child whose life is endangered?* As we write this, the newspapers are reporting the case of a couple who have decided not to consent to open-heart surgery for their mentally retarded son because then he would possibly outlive them and require institutional care for many years. Similar cases are reported from time to time. Considering this, Amram and Jochebed's experience is not so far removed from situations faced by couples today. They decided to use extraordinary means to save their child because they saw he was a fine or special child. Many people have attempted to explain this by saying that he was beautiful, or exceptionally healthy, or was marked in an unusual way so that they knew he should be saved.

   It seems to me that Moses was marked by his parents' faith. They were trusting God to provide a deliverer. Their eyes of faith saw this child as the promised one. They evidently had looked at Aaron with eyes of faith too, as he was saved only three years before. They knew God could and would use their children. Believing parents today can view each of their children as potential powers to be used by the Lord. Each is worth saving.

2. *Does persecution generally weaken or strengthen family ties? Why?* It can do either. Individuals may become obsessed with their own safety and well-being even at the expense of family members. Jesus spoke of the persecution of the saints and said, "You will be betrayed by parents, brothers, relatives and friends, and they will put some of you to death" (Luke 21:16).

   I agree with Bob, though, who says, "The promise that the 'family that prays together stays together' applies especially in times of persecution. Hard times, when death threatens, draw us together and make us concerned for one another. False values and useless competition are abandoned." From reports of the Holocaust, in which millions of Jews were killed, we learn that family ties were strengthened in persecution, making the heartbreak of separation and death even harder to bear.

3. *Compare Pharaoh's ideas about killing babies before they drew a breath with pro-abortion reasoning today.* If it is true, as I have suggested (see question 5 of "Questions for Personal Study"), that Pharaoh hoped to avoid a revolt by justifying his population control with the reasoning that it was not murder because the child that had not breathed was not a living person, then this reasoning is remarkably like the reasoning of pro-abortionists today who claim that an unborn baby is not a true person. In this way they reason that early abortion is not murder. Not all will agree with my interpretation, but it should stimulate meaningful discussion of the abortion issue.

4. *Many countries permit abortion on demand. How do you*

suppose people would react if they were told they had *to submit to abortion or kill their tiny babies?* The Hebrews evidently did not obey Pharaoh's decree to kill their babies because they continued to multiply. When life is threatened by government decrees, it suddenly becomes more precious. This is borne out by the involvement of human rights groups as they attempt to prevent the execution of criminals. These same groups are *not* usually involved in trying to save the innocent lives at stake in elective abortion.

5. *If children are a great blessing and reward from the Lord, should Christians go along with today's trend to limit family size?* This question is based on question 6 of the "Questions for Personal Study" in which we learned that God rewarded the midwives, Shiphrah and Puah, with children of their own. This fact certainly points out for us the wonderful, gracious love of God in blessing a marriage with children. These midwives saved children, and God appropriately blessed them with children. Today many couples are deciding to use birth control for selfish or materialistic reasons. They don't want to invest their time and money or themselves in the bearing or training of children because it will limit their personal or career development.

However, blessings carry responsibilities, and God requires us to think and act in faith with His guidance. Money is also a blessing, but that does not mean we should devote ourselves to getting as much of it as we can. Work is a blessing, but that does not mean we should become "workaholics." Marriage is a blessing, but that does not mean we should marry many people to get more "blessings."

It must also be pointed out that marriage does imply

the charge and privilege to have children if possible. It is the structure or context which God provided for the continuance of the human race and also the growth of the church as believing parents train their children in the Lord's way and confront them with the call to salvation. This takes a great personal commitment to and investment in marriage and parenting. Some people willingly forego the blessing of marriage or having children because it will hinder their service of the Lord. They forego these blessings as a personal sacrifice for the Lord. See Jesus' comments in Matthew 19:1–12, especially verses 11 and 12.

Bob also points out that the Bible does not condemn anyone for not having children. (Onan's sin [Gen. 38:8–10] was his refusal to keep the law because the child would not be his legally.) Rather, the many case histories of childlessness in the Bible focus on the grief of couples who could not have children.

These ideas may prove helpful as couples face this matter, seeking the will of God for their lives. The next question deals with another aspect of this subject.

6. *If you were suffering severe persecution, would you want to have a large family? Consider 1 Corinthians 7:25–28.* Jesus, when predicting the fall of Jerusalem and the end of the age, said, "How dreadful it will be in those days for pregnant women and nursing mothers!" (Matt. 24:19). The agony of having their children tortured or leaving them helpless has sometimes caused Christians to renounce their faith. Certainly grief has been multiplied by the responsibilities of marriage or parenthood in times of persecution. Paul recognized this when he said, "Because of the present crisis, I think that it is good for you to remain as you are" (1 Cor. 7:26).

The other side of this matter comes through in the study of Amram and Jochebed. Their faith enabled them to see deliverance coming—possibly through their children—and they bore and trained their children without fear. That same faith was later found in their son: "He persevered because he saw him who is invisible" (Heb. 11:27). Their eyes were focused not on their own helplessness, but on God, "our Help in ages past, our Hope for years to come."

7. *If you knew you would have your children with you for only five years or less, what effect would it have on the way you train them?* This question may be expanded to include the parent who has only a limited time to live. I had a dear Christian friend who knew she would soon die and leave her husband and three young sons. She told me she wanted me to meet them so that I could pray for them through the years after her death. She did everything she could to live her faith in her remaining years and to love and train her sons and give them a proper value system.

We agree that if we knew we could have our children for only five years or less, we would take every opportunity to teach them about the Lord—we would create opportunities to do this! We would live for the Lord more consciously. We would pray for our children and with them. We do this faithfully now, but we admit that the time limit would hone our dedication to this task.

8. *If you lived in a communist country and were forbidden to give your children religious education and you chose to disobey, how would you go about training them?* This very question should inspire us to pray for our fellow Christians who risk personal danger or even the seizure of their children if they train them to be practicing

Christians. If we were forbidden to indoctrinate our children with overt teaching, we could certainly train them by *living* our faith and by speaking of it as our personal experience. Children in their formative years want to pattern themselves after their parents. Though they may rebel against their parents' values in adolescence, they usually return to them in their mature years (Prov. 22:6). Repression forced Jochebed to be creative in her rescue of Moses, and it certainly made her creative and effective in her training of Moses, Aaron, and Miriam. God grants wisdom to parents under persecution and blesses their efforts.

9. *How can the church minister effectively to preschoolers?* The church as an organized body of believers gathered into congregations can do many things to minister to preschoolers. Here are some suggestions:
   — Have children's sermons as part of the worship service.
   — Include their needs in congregational prayers.
   — Have Bible stories and songs instead of just nursery care or playtime for three to five year olds.
   — Establish Christian day-care centers.

10. *What suggestions do you have for couples who must be separated much of the time, thus causing one to have more involvement in the training of their children than the other?* Through the years, Bob and I have been separated many times for periods of several weeks when his job required advanced training. Some couples are separated by long-term illnesses, service commitments, jail terms, or jobs requiring extensive travel. These separations place stress on the marriage and family. Group members may have suggestions to help such couples. Prayer is essential—for wisdom, patience, understand-

ing, and strength against temptation. Communication with each other and with the children is essential. Writing may be a tiresome burden, but it provides relief and introspection for the one who writes, and personal love, concern, and involvement for the one who receives. Telephones are blessings. Bob suggests that the mate at home keep a journal with notations of high or low points in family life so that decisions can be made together on problems and the context that spawned them can be remembered.

We have seen another aspect of marriage as presented in a Bible case history. Again we have seen God's ruling hand in all the events that shaped the lives of His people. Surely this account of Amram and Jochebed is recorded to build our faith for trials we may face and to open our hearts in an awareness of the suffering that fellow Christians must endure.

8

ZECHARIAH AND ELIZABETH

BIBLE PASSAGE

Luke 1

OBJECTIVES

1. To become better acquainted with Zechariah and Elizabeth and to learn why the Lord chose them to be the parents of John the Baptist.
2. To evaluate John's work.
3. To consider the effects of childlessness on a marriage.
4. To understand the implications of their "blameless walk" before the Lord.
5. To explore their reaction to the announcement of John's coming birth.
6. To see how God works to prepare His people for His coming—then and now.

BACKGROUND

God's people were expecting the Messiah. Many prophets had foretold His coming, but the prophecies of Daniel were given special attention. The angel Gabriel had appeared to

Daniel with a message about the time period between the decree to rebuild Jerusalem and the coming of the Anointed One. This is commonly known as the prophecy of seventy weeks and is recorded in Daniel 9:20–27. This prophecy was interpreted as 490 years, dating from the rebuilding of Jerusalem in 538-495 B.C. Those who were truly longing for the Messiah were filled with hope.

Zechariah was a priest, a member of the eighth company of priests—the Abijah group—descended from Aaron, the first high priest. King David had set up a schedule of service for the priestly families so that each would have a turn to serve for one week, two times in a year, in the temple. This is recorded in 1 Chronicles 24:1–18. Zechariah was on duty when introduced in Luke 1. Once in a priest's lifetime he could be chosen to burn incense, representing the prayers and praise of God's people, before the golden altar. When this great honor was given to Zechariah, the angel Gabriel appeared to him to tell him that the time had come for prophecy to be fulfilled.

Elizabeth was also a direct descendant of Aaron. She was named after Aaron's wife, Elisheba (Exod. 6:23). Her name means "I worship God" or "God is an oath." She met the requirements not only for a priest's wife (Lev. 21:7), but also for a high priest's wife (Lev. 21:13–15).

Zechariah and Elizabeth were perhaps in their sixties as we meet them. Zechariah told the angel, "I am an old man and my wife is well along in years" (Luke 1:18). They had longed and prayed for a child, and at this point in life it seemed impossible that their prayers would ever be answered. The facts are stated starkly in Luke 1:7: "But they had no children, because Elizabeth was barren; and they were both well along in years."

It is unlikely that Zechariah and Elizabeth lived to see their son, John, baptize Jesus, the Messiah, and they were probably spared the agony of learning of their son's tragic death (Matt. 14:1–13). But they continued to walk before the Lord blamelessly, living by faith in God who keeps His promises.

QUESTIONS FOR PERSONAL STUDY

1. *What qualities was God looking for in parents for John the Baptist?* It is clear from numerous examples in Scripture that the leaders of God's people were prepared for their task by being trained and nurtured by God-fearing parents. This, then, was the most important quality. We may be sure that God chose parents who were firm, loving, understanding, and who lived a triumphant faith in God and His promise. Also, Luke 1 emphasizes that they were from the line of Aaron. I believe God chose a priestly family to prepare the way for Jesus because the priests brought the prayers of the people to God. John was the "Amen, Come Lord Jesus" at the end of centuries of prayer for the Deliverer, prayers offered for the people by the priests.

2. *How did Zechariah react to the angel's message (Luke 1:12, 18, 20)?* Bob says, "He was startled, gripped with fear. He could not believe it without a sign." We are reminded of the believers in the early church who were praying for Peter's release from prison, but who could not believe Rhoda when she said Peter was at the door (Acts 12:13–16). We are often like them and like Zechariah: we pray earnestly, but retain a portion of doubt that God will choose to grant our requests—especially when it seems impossible to us.

3. *How did Elizabeth react to the news (Luke 1:25)?* She

gave God the glory for working the miracle in her, recognizing this as an answer to her personal prayers. It was always a disgrace for Hebrew women to be barren because then they did not fit into the social structure and they did not have the hope that their child would be the Promised One. Rachel expressed the same sentiment when Joseph was born, "God has taken away my disgrace" (Gen. 30:23).

4. *What do you learn about Elizabeth in Luke 1:41–45?* Elizabeth was filled with the Holy Spirit and became a prophetess. No one knew about Mary's pregnancy yet; the Spirit revealed it to Elizabeth in her unborn child's response to the presence of the embryonic Jesus. She spoke in a surge of joy, excitement, faith, and humility. She was the first person—even before the Virgin Mary—to confess Jesus as Lord in the flesh. She did this in the power of the Holy Spirit, just as Peter did when he confessed, "'You are the Christ, the son of the living God.' Jesus replied, 'Blessed are you, Simon son of Jonah, for this was not revealed to you by man, but by my Father in heaven'" (Matt. 16:16–17).

Many commentators observe that Elizabeth, though she was much older than Mary, readily acknowledged Mary's great honor. She expressed joy and wonder and no bitterness or regret that a younger woman was chosen to bear the Messiah.

5. *What do you learn about Zechariah from his song (Luke 1:67–79)?* Zechariah, filled with the Holy Spirit, had such great faith that he viewed salvation as an accomplished fact. Bob noticed that Zechariah was well-trained in knowledge of the Law and Prophets. This knowledge gave him a clear understanding of John's work as a prophet. Zechariah composed this song him-

self. Elizabeth could well have sung Psalm 113.

6. *Why were the neighbors and relatives involved in the circumcising and naming of the child (Luke 1:57–63)?* These verses make this story live for us. We know how relatives, neighbors, and friends are usually involved in our lives, especially when a child is born. We see a similar situation in Ruth 4:16–17 when the neighbor women commented on the birth and named the child.

When our last child was born (nine-and-a-half years after the previous child), everyone rejoiced with us. We received over a hundred congratulatory cards. When people learned that we had named her Mary, they immediately asked, "Is she named after your mothers?" When we named our first daughter Bethel Joy, most people wanted to know why we had chosen that name.

This type of interest was intensified when John the Baptist was born. His father's temple experience and sudden dumbness and the age of his parents all generated interest and joy. Circumcision was a sacrament, not a secular or private event, so many were present for the ceremony.

As far as we know, Zechariah was not struck with deafness, but the excited neighbors made signs to him, asking about the baby's name. Imagine their astonishment when he wrote "His name is John" and then, after nine months of silence, broke into a song of praise and prophecy!

Every one of those neighbors and relatives was gathered there by God for a purpose: to make them witnesses of the Lord's miracle and to create expectation for further evidence of the Lord's work.

7. *What did John's birth do for his parents (Luke 1:14)?* Joy and delight became a part of their life as they watched him grow and trained him for the Lord's service.

8. *John means "the grace of Jehovah." Why was this a good name for him?* John's work signaled the beginning of the dispensation of grace. God was now about to fulfill His promise of salvation.

9. *How did John's work prepare the people for the coming of the Messiah (Luke 1:16–17; 3:1–20)?* Though the Jews were expecting the Messiah, there were many rival, antagonistic sects (Luke 6:15; Acts 5:35–37). People also were caught in the grip of materialism. Before people can come into the presence of God, they must be cleansed—just as the Israelites had to purify themselves for three days before God came to them on Mount Sinai. John's call to reconciliation and repentance and his baptizing were part of the purification process required for people who were to be introduced to the Son of God.

10. *How was John like Elijah? See 1 Kings 18–19; Malachi 4:5–6; Matthew 11:1–6; Luke 1:16–17.* John was not a reincarnation of Elijah, but like Elijah, he was equipped by the Holy Spirit for a great prophetic task. Both called the people back to the true worship of God. Both preached reconciliation and repentance. Both frequented the wilderness. Both experienced a time when they doubted their calling and the validity of their work.

11. *What do you learn in Luke 3:1–20 and Acts 18:24–28; 19:1–12 about the effectiveness of John's work?* Many people from many walks of life heard John's fearless preaching. They repented and sought to live changed lives. One young man, Apollos, who was converted by John the Baptist became a powerful preacher of the gospel. Paul found a group of believers in Ephesus who had been converted by John; they were happy to believe in Jesus.

12. *What was Jesus' evaluation of John and his work (Matt.*

11:1–15)? Jesus stated that from the days of John the Baptist the kingdom of heaven advanced forcefully. This means that John had done a good job as the "announcer" of Christ. Jesus also gave the highest tribute to John, saying, "Among those born of women there has not risen anyone greater than John the Baptist." Bob adds, "I am struck by Christ's next statement: 'yet he who is least in the kingdom of heaven is greater than he' (Matt. 11:11). How many of us are interested in being least in the kingdom of heaven? What glory awaits the humble ones who serve the Lord!"

QUESTIONS FOR GROUP DISCUSSION

1. *How many instances can you think of in the Bible where sterile couples became parents of a special child?* This question is intended to get discussion started. Members may mention Abraham and Sarah, Isaac and Rebekah, Jacob and Rachel, Samson's parents, Elkanah and Hannah, and others.
2. *Why would God choose to work in this way?* Bob answers, "He shows that He is truly God. He does what man cannot do. He does the impossible. He humbles people." God calls attention to the child because of the remarkable circumstances of its birth. The child's parents grow in faith in their time of testing, and as they have no other children, the mother can give full attention to the care and training of this long-hoped-for child.
3. *How can the disappointed longing for a child affect a marriage?* This trial can draw a couple closer together and closer to God. Or, as Bob says, "It can make them feel incomplete. Each partner can feel guilty of inade-

quacy, and too often the word 'fault' is used, pointing to one or the other as the cause of the disappointment. This can drive a wedge into the unity of marriage and cause loneliness, hurt, and separation."

4. *Notice the tribute to Zechariah and Elizabeth in Luke 1:6. Does this mean they were happily married? Explain.* Some group members may point out that marriage partners may be individually zealous in serving the Lord and busy in many kingdom activities, but not happily married. A happy marriage involves not only commitment to Christ, but also commitment to one another.

In answer to this, it may be pointed out that true commitment to God involves obedience to His Word. This Word commands us to love one another. The Word of God portrays marriage as being like the relationship between Christ and the church (Eph. 5:22–33; Rev. 19:6–8). It stresses love and commitment to one another. Those who serve the Lord *together* have a very happy marriage. We know!

5. *Is fear unbelief? See Luke 1:12–13, 20, 29–34; 2:9–10.* When reading Luke 1, many people conclude that Zechariah was struck dumb because he had been afraid of the angel. But in reading the other passages we learn that others experienced a natural fear when visited by angels and were not condemned for it. In fact, throughout the Bible we are told to "fear the Lord." Fear is not unbelief.

Zechariah harbored some unbelief that the angel could detect in his words (Luke 1:18, 20) or attitude, and so he was given a sign as he requested. The sign was dumbness—hard to bear when he had such great news to tell, but also a merciful assurance that he really did see and hear God's angel promise them a son.

6. *Why was Zechariah struck dumb until he named the baby?* As we said above, the sign confirmed for Zechariah the angel's appearance and message. "Also," says Bob, "God wanted to show the world that He was in control and that He was real. This sign made Zechariah and God the 'talk of the town.'" The naming of the baby was an act of obedience. It was a reaffirmation of Zechariah's faith and released him from muteness to voluble praise.

7. *Why did Elizabeth hide herself (Luke 1:24)?* Many answers may be given. Any woman who finds herself unexpectedly pregnant needs time to adjust to the idea. An older woman knows she will be the focus of much attention and the subject of many jokes. This is hard to reconcile with her intimate wonder at the creative work going on in her body. Besides, Elizabeth must have wanted to savor the spiritual experience of God's miraculous answer to her prayers.

John Calvin speaks of her great faith and points out that a greater spiritual impact would be made on others if she were suddenly discovered to be pregnant only a few months before the birth. "For, when the works of God show themselves gradually, in process of time we make less account of them than if the thing had been accomplished all at once, without our having ever heard of it. It was not, therefore, on her own account, but rather with a view to others, that Elizabeth *hid herself.*"[1]

8. *Why did God bring Mary and Elizabeth together?* This was an act of God's love and understanding. He knew that Elizabeth and Mary would need reassurance, under-

---

[1]John Calvin, *Commentary on a Harmony of the Evangelists, Matthew, Mark and Luke,* tr. by Rev. William Pringle (Grand Rapids: Wm. B. Eerdmans, 1949), 1:30.

standing, and encouragement in their unique pregnancies.

When the angel left Mary and she stood there wondering if this could really have happened to her, she remembered the words of the angel telling her Elizabeth was going to have a child in her old age. "For nothing is impossible with God" (Luke 1:37). Mary claimed this news as a sign from God that she truly had been chosen to be the mother of the Messiah. She was further assured when she heard Elizabeth call her the mother of the Lord before she had an opportunity to share her secret.

Elizabeth was filled with the Holy Spirit and thrilled when she felt her unborn child acknowledge the presence of the embryonic Savior.

For three months these expectant mothers were spiritually strengthened as they marveled together at the grace and power of God.

Bob says, "They could share their joys and their secrets and the wonder of it all."

9. *What verse (or verses) in Luke 1 comforts you?* This question provides an opportunity for group members to share what the Spirit has been teaching them in this lesson. I chose the obvious verse, "For nothing is impossible with God" (Luke 1:37). Bob chose the beautiful verse from Mary's song, "His mercy extends to those who fear him, from generation to generation" (Luke 1:50).

10. *How can couples today prepare the way for the Lord's second coming in their own lives and in the training of their children? See Luke 1:17; 3:7–18.* We must recognize sin and be cleansed so that we can come into the presence of God.

    — We must strive for reconciliation, especially in parent-child relationships (Luke 1:17).

— We may not rest our hope for salvation on the fact that our ancestors were believers (Luke 3:8).
— We must show fruit—evidence—in our lives that we are forgiven sinners (Luke 3:9).
— We must share our material blessings with others (Luke 3:11).
— We must be just (Luke 3:13).
— We must be content (Luke 3:14).

Bob was impressed by the tone of judgment in John's words as they apply to us too. Judgment Day is coming. We must repent. We must each, personally, trust in Jesus for salvation. We must show the fruits of thankfulness in our lives. Every day is "show and tell" day for Christians.

Prepared people can say, "Come, Lord Jesus!"

9

MOSES AND ZIPPORAH

BIBLE PASSAGES

Exodus 2:11–25; 3:1–12; 4:18–26; 18; Numbers
10:29–34; 12:1–3

OBJECTIVES

1. To discover God's purpose in sending Moses to Midian.
2. To evaluate Moses' relationship with his wife and her family.
3. To explore the spiritual differences and backgrounds of Moses and Zipporah.
4. To try to understand the reasons for Moses' near death experience at the inn.
5. To learn why this incident led to their marital separation and to observe their reunion.
6. To discuss the relative importance of office and marriage.
7. To consider the contribution to (or lack of interest in) marriage by one whose attention is largely diverted to some other cause.
8. To discuss needs of wives and families of church leaders and how they may be ministered to.

9. To evaluate the marriage of Moses and Zipporah.
10. To determine God's purpose in recording this circumcision incident in the Bible.

BACKGROUND

God's people were suffering as slaves in Egypt. The Pharaoh who "did not know about Joseph" (Exod. 1:8) was afraid of the potential power of the Hebrews should they decide to revolt. Moses was born after the law was passed that all Hebrew boy babies were to be killed. The decision of his parents and God's wonderful provision is studied in the lesson on Amram and Jochebed.

Moses was brought up in the palace as the son of a princess, but he identified with his blood-family, the Hebrews. At the age of forty, he killed an Egyptian who was beating a Hebrew and hid the body in the sand. He learned that his act had been observed when he tried to break up a fight between two Hebrews and one asked, "Who made you ruler and judge over us? Are you thinking of killing me as you killed the Egyptian?" (Exod. 2:14).

Moses had to flee for his life. He was not ready to lead the people, and they were not ready to accept him as their leader. God sent him to Midianite "graduate school" where for forty years he studied "patience" and "desert survival."

QUESTIONS FOR PERSONAL STUDY

1. *Read the passages listed above. From Moses' viewpoint, why did he go to Midian?* Moses went to Midian to escape from Pharaoh who wanted to kill him. He was a

fugitive because he had killed an Egyptian. Midian was out of Pharaoh's jurisdiction so Moses was safe there.

From God's viewpoint, why did Moses have to go to Midian? Moses was not ready to lead God's people. He had to learn patience. He had to learn to depend completely on God. He had to learn desert survival in the very area where he would one day lead the people. He had to meet Jethro who would be his teacher and advisor, and he had to teach Jethro about the Lord.

Two things are interesting to notice. First, imagine Moses as a young man, brought up in the luxury of the palace. He did not know the true meaning of suffering so he could not identify with God's people as they suffered. The nomadic life of a Midianite shepherd certainly provided a growth experience for him.

Second, we see him arrive at the well just as the young women were about to draw water for the flocks. This is the third time we read of this happening: Abraham's servant met Rebekah at the well (Gen. 24:11), and Jacob met Rachel at the well (Gen. 29:2). Later, Jesus met a woman at a well and brought her salvation (John 4).

2. *What are the two names given for Moses' father-in-law (Exod. 2:18; 3:1)?* The names are Reuel and Jethro. One could have been his family name and the other an official name. We do not know why two names are given, but they clearly refer to the same person. See also Numbers 10:29.

3. *Jethro was a Midianite priest. From whom did the Midianites descend (Gen. 25:1–6)?* Midian was the son of Abraham and Keturah. The Genesis passage pointedly says that Keturah's sons were sent away from Isaac, indicating that they were not to be included with Isaac's

descendants who were chosen to receive special blessings and to bring forth the Redeemer.

4. *Could Jethro and Zipporah have known the importance of circumcision as a sign of God's covenant (Gen. 17:9–14)?* Abraham was commanded by God to circumcise all the males in his household. This command was also to be kept by all of Abraham's descendants, including Midian and Jethro.

5. *Moses did not tell Jethro about the real reason for his return to Egypt. He just packed up his family and went. How do you suppose Zipporah may have felt about this trip?* This question is meant to help us understand Zipporah's feelings. It may have been exciting and challenging for her to go on this journey, but more likely it was a time of grief and apprehension. Most wives are nervous about meeting their husband's family, especially when he is of a different nationality, culture, and religion. Zipporah must have felt these qualms, but in addition she had to leave her own family, perhaps forever, and she had to make a long difficult journey with two small sons to care for in primitive travel conditions. (Isn't it surprising, though, that there were inns along the way for travelers in those days?) Many wives today quiver when faced with a long difficult trip with small children. As we study this lesson, which gives us more information about Moses than Zipporah, we must try to understand her position.

6. *What does Exodus 4:20 suggest about the ages of the children?* Since Moses' wife and two sons could travel on one donkey, the children must have been very young. Evidently, then, the child's circumcision had not been postponed for a long period of time.

7. *When Moses was near death, why did Zipporah circum-*

cise their son? The Bible doesn't give us much information in this strange and difficult passage. In some way God made it clear that Moses' illness was a punishment for disobedience. Zipporah must have performed the circumcision to save her husband's life.

8. *What does Zipporah's statement "You are a bridegroom of blood" indicate (Exod. 4:25–26)?* Bob feels this statement expressed a resentment and rejection of the Hebrew religion with its "theology of blood." I sense that her oldest son's circumcision had been repulsive to her—it was bloody and it hurt him, and it may have seemed like mutilation to her. Evidently she had no appreciation of its spiritual significance and was not interested in having her second son marked as one belonging to the Lord who had promised wonderful things to His people.

9. *What was the probable result of this argument (Exod. 4:26; 18:2–4)?* Apparently Moses was healed and decided to go on to Egypt without his family; he sent them back to Midian to be cared for by Jethro.

10. *Was Moses glad to see Jethro bringing Zipporah and his sons to him (Exod. 18:5–9)?* We don't know how happy he was to see his wife and children, but we assume he was happy because of his warm greeting to Jethro. This chapter gives us insight into the love Moses felt for Jethro who had taken him, a stranger, not only into his home and business, but also into his family. It seems that through Moses, Jethro became a true believer in God. We conclude this because of his confession (Exod. 18:10–11) and the fact that God accepted his sacrifice and approved of his advice to Moses.

Moses must have loved and been loved by all his wife's family. In Numbers 10:29–34 we learn that he urged her brother to join Israel and receive the promise. When Hobab refused, Moses pleaded that they needed his expertise and wilderness knowledge. Apparently Hobab joined the people of the Lord and served as their guide and scout.

11. *Who was "first lady" for the Israelites (Exod. 15:20; Num. 12:1–3)?* These passsages and Micah 6:4 indicate that Miriam, the prophetess, older sister of Aaron and Moses, was the female leader of the Hebrew nation.

12. *If the wife mentioned in Numbers 12:1 was Zipporah, what could have caused Miriam to complain?* No one knows for sure if this was Zipporah. Many commentators agree with the historian Josephus that Zipporah had died and Moses had married an Ethiopian woman. Some make much of the fact that this could have been a racially mixed marriage.

On the other hand, according to Genesis 2:13 the land of Cush was near what was later called Mesopotamia; therefore, "Cushite" could have referred to nomadic Midianites, Zipporah's people.

The problem which surfaced in Numbers 12 was an underlying jealousy of Moses' recognition as leader of God's people. The outburst was prompted by Moses' wife. It seems most likely that Moses' wife was of a different culture and religion—that he was unequally yoked to an unbeliever (2 Cor. 6:14)—and Miriam and Aaron felt this disqualified him as a leader.

Others have pointed out that Zipporah may have been a bitter, resentful, outspoken woman (Exod. 4:24–26) who opposed Miriam and Aaron and eroded Moses' authority and happiness.

QUESTIONS FOR GROUP DISCUSSION

1. *Was Moses a courageous man (Exod. 2:11–14, 17; 4:10, 13)?* Moses seems to have been courageous but cautious in his defense of the Hebrew slave. He was naturally afraid when he learned that Pharaoh was after him. He was brave when he came to the aid of the shepherd girls. He was not courageous when the Lord commissioned him to go to Pharaoh.

   Bob says, "Moses seems to have been courageous in physical struggles, but he felt very inferior when it came to defending himself or others with words."

   God was angry with Moses, but He met his need and sent Aaron as his helper (Exod. 4:14–16). God's strength overcame Moses' weakness. We can be encouraged as we see God's patience with Moses in this incident.

2. *What kind of wife did Moses need?* We believe that in his years of exile, he needed a wife to make a home away from home for him. He needed comfort and love and encouragement. He found these in Jethro's home. Jethro gave him his daughter to supply these needs.

   Later, Moses needed a wife who could appreciate his concern for his people, a true helper to him as he carried out his calling to be a deliverer and spiritual leader. Zipporah did not fit the needs of this period of his life, but he did not divorce her.

3. *Why do you suppose Moses' son had not been circumcised?* Bob answers, "Apparently Moses and Zipporah had disagreed on this matter either because of their differing religious convictions or because she did not want to shed the child's blood. Moses was a man who could not win a battle of words, so he gave up trying to convince Zipporah that this should be done." Others have

suggested that the rite was forgotten in the excitement of
the journey, but Zipporah's bitter words suggest a dis-
agreement or at least a reluctance on her part to have the
child circumcised.

4. *Why was it so important for him to be circumcised that
   God brought Moses to the point of death?* Bob says,
   "God required that Moses, the lawgiver, obey the law.
   Moses also had to be the spiritual leader in his family,
   and he had not been."

   In thinking about circumcision as the Old Testament
   identification mark of God's covenant promise, I see that
   Moses had to mark his child by the shedding of blood.
   This pointed ahead to the Savior who would come and
   save His people by the shedding of His blood.

   Also, I see this incident as a battle between good and
   evil. Zipporah served false gods. Her influence was
   powerful, and Satan could triumph if a son of the spiritual
   leader of Israel was led into paganism instead of
   Yahwism. We are given insight into the seriousness
   of this matter when we read Numbers 22:1–7; 25; 31.
   We learn that when Balaam was unable to curse Israel,
   he suggested that the Midianites and Moabites weaken
   Israel through intermarriage (see Rev. 2:14). This proved
   to be a real threat to the spiritual purity of the nation
   and was severely punished, the Midianites being all
   but wiped out. Moses, himself married to a Midianite
   who tried to keep him from obeying the law, knew the
   dangers of intermarriage. God required that Moses be
   above reproach so that he could fight this battle with
   Satan.

5. *In what way could Moses' preoccupation with the needs
   of his people have interfered with his marriage relationship?* As things were going, Moses would have had no

time or mental and emotional energy to give to a family. This was evident to Jethro soon after he arrived in camp with Zipporah and her sons. Through Jethro, God showed Moses a solution to the problem by encouraging him to delegate some of the duties and authority to other capable people. This demonstrates God's interest in the quality of family life enjoyed by His people.

6. *Which was more important, Moses' office or his marriage? Explain.* This is a difficult question. The Bible passages seem to infer that his office was more important because he served and led so many people. He had to put the needs of God's people before his own needs and the needs of his family.

7. *Does the description of Moses as a meek man (Num. 12:3) help us understand his marital problems? Explain.* Some people equate meek with weak. They believe Moses was overpowered by his wife. Moses *does* seem to have been a man who did not enjoy problems or confrontations, and this may have led to his difficulty with Zipporah over the circumcision. But when Moses is described as more meek than anyone on earth, it is referring to his humility, not weakness. Moses had learned his unworthiness and his utter dependence upon God. When a person's willful nature is harnessed for God's service, and when he recognizes that all his strength and ability come from God alone, he is meek. God's strength is his, and he is then by no means weak.

8. *How could his marriage experiences have helped Moses as a leader?* Bob says, "Any time you have to deal with problems and difficulties in life you grow in knowledge, in understanding, and in dependence on God." Moses learned to understand family and marital problems and the dangers of intermarriage. This helped him as a judge

and as a leader. (Refer to the answer given with question 4 of this section.)

9. *How would you describe the marriage of Moses and Zipporah?* Bob answers, "I think Moses was happy that Jethro took him in and gave him Zipporah. I am sure they had happy times, but their differences caused difficulties." I do not think this was a happy marriage. Moses was not an enthusiastic husband, and Zipporah, given as a gift by her father, was bitter and resentful.

10. *Should church members be more understanding of the needs of and stresses borne by pastors' wives and families?* This lesson evokes sympathy for Zipporah as well as impatience with her. She seems to have been a pawn with little to say about her life. Hers was probably a lonely life. She was set apart from the people by her marriage to Moses and was expected to be a model person if not a contributor to their religion and culture. Everything was foreign to her, and we can understand that she might have resented the fact that her husband was possessed by the people.

    Many pastors' wives and families are in the same plight today. They may be isolated, lonely, and expected to live perfect lives. Often the pastor is so busy that his wife has to be "father and mother" to the children. Group members may suggest practical ways to approach and alleviate this problem.

11. *Many marriages are shaken by the dedication of one of the spouses to career interests (e.g., the high divorce rate among people involved in the space program). How should Christians deal with this problem?* Bob says, "The Christian must recognize his responsibility to his family and give them his love and devotion. He must also work at his calling wholeheartedly (Col. 3:23–24). This calls

for balance and wisdom, and we must depend on God for this."

The importance of the marriage relationship is affirmed in the example of Christ as head or husband of the church (Eph. 5:21–33). While the importance of dedication to a career of service is demonstrated in Moses' life, we should note that Moses overloaded himself and that God showed him a way out of this dilemma just at the time when his responsibilities to wife and family became more demanding (Exod. 18:13–27).

With prayer, we too can find ways to divide work and delegate responsibility. It is important to take time to strengthen the marriage bond, and it is important to spend time with children, especially in their formative years. We must ask God to give us wisdom to decide what is really important so that in all things we may honor Him and walk in His way.

10

MR. AND MRS. MANOAH

BIBLE PASSAGES

Judges 13–14

OBJECTIVES

1. To see that Samson was set apart for special service.
2. To study the parents God provided for Samson, noting their spiritual commitment and the strength of their marriage.
3. To learn how they handled perplexing events in life.
4. To discuss the handling of similar situations today.
5. To find comfort and encouragement for parents today.

BACKGROUND

Mr. and Mrs. Manoah lived with fear and repression. The Hebrews had not fully conquered the Promised Land, and they were poorly organized to fight against the pagan nations who resented their presence. The Philistines had harassed the

Hebrews for many years, taking their weapons and crops. The worship of God was deteriorating due to difficult distances and the corrupt leadership of Eli's sons.

Add to this Mr. and Mrs. Manoah's disappointment and disgrace at having no children, and the picture is quite dismal. Yet there was love. We know Manoah loved his wife because he could have divorced her for barrenness, but he chose to suffer with her instead. They communicated with each other freely. Manoah was a protective husband who prayed over problems. Noting the many plural personal pronouns in Judges 13:8–23, we feel their unity and we see that the fear of the Lord was in them.

They named their son Samson which is derived from the word "shemesh" meaning *sun*. His name may be translated *strength of the sun*. This reminds us of Psalm 84:11: "For the Lord God is a sun and shield." His name was a statement of their faith in their son's divine calling.

Samson was not a judge in the sense that he heard complaints and defenses and then ruled on them. Instead, he was used as a vindicator of God's people, bringing justice and judgment from God. He did this work independently and sporadically, possibly during the time that Eli was the spiritual leader of the Hebrews.

QUESTIONS FOR PERSONAL STUDY

1. *What is a Nazirite (Num. 6:1–21)?* This word is often spelled "Nazarite" and is often confused with "Nazarene." The NIV spelling we use here is preferable because it is based on the Hebrew word "nazir" which means *consecrated* or *dedicated*.

   The passage from Numbers tells us that a Nazirite was

someone who had taken a vow and separated himself from ordinary life for special service for the Lord. His dedication was seen by others in three ways: he did not drink wine, he did not cut his hair, and he did not make himself unclean for worship by contacting death in any way.

2. *What is suggested by the fact that this separation was put into effect before Samson's birth?* Samson's consecration was lifelong and began with his conception; he was guarded from contamination even before birth. Another possibility is that his mother's pregnancy was a time of consecration for her to prepare for the task of bringing up this special child.

3. *What was Samson's lifework to be (Judg. 13:5)?* Today many young people struggle with career choices. Samson never had that problem. His life and work were decided for him before his birth. He was to be the arm of God's justice. He was to begin the deliverance of Israel from the Philistines. Baby Samson represented hope for God's people. His birth announcement and the visible signs of his separation for service bolstered the faith of God's people, assuring them that God had heard their cry and would save them. This is why Samson was listed with the heroes of faith in Hebrews 11.

4. *Why was he to be a Nazirite?* The Nazirite vow bound him to God and separated him from a normal life. His long hair was a topic for conversation and made him noticeable.

   Wine dulled the senses. Because the deliverer of Israel had to have a clear mind as he brought God's justice, he was required to abstain from this or other fermented drink. See also Proverbs 31:4–7.

   Unclean foods were identified with sin and impurity

and made a person unfit for worship—for appearing in the presence of God. Samson represented God; thus, he had to stay pure.

(It is possible that Samson drank wine at the wedding feast [Judg. 14:10]. He also became unclean when he took honey out of the carcass of the lion [Judg. 14:8–9]. He was overcome by a temptress, and his hair was cut [Judg. 16:19]. Samson suffered for these sins, yet God heard his prayer, forgave him, and used him once more. We see God's forgiveness and are encouraged as we review our own sins and weaknesses.

Also, there is a paradox here. Samson was not to contact death, yet his mission was to kill. In this I see him as a type of Christ who became sin for us—became totally contaminated and unclean—that God's justice might be satisfied and we might be set free.)

5. *The angel came to Mrs. Manoah and later talked to her husband too (Judg. 13:11–14). Why was it good for both of them to know about the coming birth and the Nazirite vow?* Both of them had to be impressed with Samson's calling and his vow. They had to work together to train him. It would have been difficult for the wife to take on the Nazirite vow and raise her son as a Nazirite without her husband's understanding and cooperation.

6. *Did the Manoahs believe the message (Judg. 13:8–9, 12, 15, 17)?* They both believed. This is evident in Mr. Manoah's prayer and their wanting to honor the messenger. Bob says, "They believed the message, but did not immediately recognize the messenger as the angel of the Lord."

7. *What can we learn from Manoah's prayer (Judg. 13:8)?* Manoah lived long before the Epistle of James was written, but he knew he could go directly to the Source of

wisdom to be equipped for the task of bringing up his child. "If any of you lacks wisdom, he should ask God, who gives generously to all without finding fault, and it will be given him" (James 1:5).

Manoah uses the plural pronoun "us," thus recognizing that parenting was a job for both father and mother. This is also expressed in Proverbs 1:8: "Listen, my son, to your father's instruction and do not forsake your mother's teaching."

8. *Who was the angel who appeared to the Manoahs (Judg. 13:8, 22; Isa. 9:6)?* This angel was Christ Jesus making an Old Testament or pre-incarnation appearance. He appeared with special messages and commissions to Abraham (Gen. 18), to Jacob (Gen. 32:22–32), and to others. We recognize Him as God Himself because He received worship. Angels were not to be worshiped (Rev. 19:9–10). "Do not let anyone who delights in false humility and the worship of angels disqualify you for the prize" (Col. 2:18). Jacob, Mr. and Mrs. Manoah, and others recognized Him as God and were afraid because they had seen Him.

In Isaiah 9:6 the word translated "Wonderful" as a name of the Messiah is the same word the angel used when Manoah asked His name (Judg. 13:18). Some versions translate this as "secret," some as "wonderful," some as "beyond understanding."

9. *What did the angel want them to understand (Judg. 13:16)?* Samson's parents had to recognize God as the source of this commission. They had to offer praise and thanksgiving to God. A similar event is recorded in Judges 6:11–24.

10. *What do you learn about Mrs. Manoah in Judges 13:23?* Bob sees this as an expression of her implicit faith in

God's word. She knew the message was true and could not be fulfilled if their lives were snuffed out. Herbert Lockyer points to this verse as evidence that she had "sanctified common sense."[1]

11. *Were Samson's parents right to arrange his marriage when they did not approve of it (Judg. 14:8–11)?* This is a subjective question which may be applied to similar situations today, and opinions may vary. This question prepares the student for question 4 of the group discussion questions.

12. *Do you think Samson understood his special calling by God (Judg. 16:17, 28; Heb. 11:32–34)?* These verses indicate that he did. I cannot help but wonder if he would have shunned moral lapses if he had seen the angel too. He learned of his calling through his parents and may have rebelled against them. "Blessed are those who have not seen and yet have believed" (John 20:29).

QUESTIONS FOR GROUP DISCUSSION

1. *What can you learn about Mr. and Mrs. Manoah's marriage from Judges 13:6–11?* Many insights may be gained from these verses. First of all, they were united in fearing the Lord. They thought of each other when decisions had to be made or news shared. They communicated well.

   Notice the contrast between the report about Mrs. Manoah that "she told her husband" (13:6) and the comment about Abigail (1 Sam. 25:19), "She told not her husband." Abigail's husband was harsh, unloving, and unkind so she dared not tell him the news she had heard.

---

[1]Herbert Lockyer, *The Women of the Bible* (Grand Rapids: Zondervan, 1967), pp. 186-187.

We may infer that Manoah was the opposite: gentle, loving, and kind.

As a woman and a wife, I appreciate the protection demonstrated by Manoah. He prayed about this remarkable event and checked it out for his wife to be sure all was well. He wanted to be included with her in the divine charge.

What excitement the message must have brought to their marriage. At last they were to be blessed with a child, a son! And not an ordinary son, but a deliverer for their suffering people. Great awe must have filled them as they were used by the Lord to bring this special child into the world.

2. *Why did God choose them to be parents of a special child?* When an unusual child is born, the parents often resent the suggestion that God chose them to have that child. They cannot feel joy at being chosen to bear suffering, disappointment, hardship, and challenge. Yet God makes no mistakes, and He makes no promises that the way of service will be without thorns. We see in this lesson that the child with a special calling is noticeable—perhaps mocked for being different. Handicapped or gifted children are noticeably different from others, are often mocked, and are often difficult to live with.

It takes true spiritual commitment to bear the strain that such a child places on a marriage. God sent Samson, John the Baptist, and others to parents who were devoted to Him and had a strong, loving marriage. He sent these special children to praying, communicating parents. He sent these children to intelligent parents who had the time and ability to give them personal attention and training for service. God works in the same way today.

3. *What could Mr. and Mrs. Manoah lean upon for comfort as they observed their son's strange life?* They must have often asked, "Why?" Then they could remind each other of the angel's visit. They knew God was working out His plan through their son.

Parents of special children today are probably thinking, "If only we had seen an angel!" Angels do not come with announcements today, but we have the Spirit and the Word of the Lord Jesus Christ who appeared to Mr. and Mrs. Manoah. The very inclusion of this story in the Bible teaches us that God works out His plan through special children.

One way He does this is by putting us in touch with other parents and children who have similar struggles. He expands our world, redefines our value system, and teaches us to trust and praise Him. "Praise be to the God and Father of our Lord Jesus Christ, the Father of compassion and the God of all comfort, who comforts us in all our troubles, so that we can comfort those in any trouble with the comfort we ourselves have received from God" (2 Cor. 1:3–4).

These words come through the Holy Spirit of Christ and are poured into our hearts. He is in us to comfort us each day. We can trust the same Angel of Jehovah who was trusted by Mr. and Mrs. Manoah.

4. *Were Samson's parents right in challenging his choice of a wife (Judg. 14:1–4)? Consult Exodus 34:15–16 and Deuteronomy 7:3–4. Explain.* The Exodus and Deuteronomy passages were God's warnings to His children. He expects us to warn our children in the same way. Bob senses the increased concern for an acceptable mate felt by parents of a special child. The separated Samson had been guarded against impurity; now he

wanted to become one with it by marrying this girl. Samson's parents were right to challenge his choice.

5. *Should Christian parents attend the wedding of their child to an unbeliever? Explain.* We believe they should. It may be difficult to accept the child's choice, but God calls us to witness for Him through love. He gives us the perfect example of a loving Father as He deals with us, His children.

6. *What can parents learn from Judges 14:4?* This is a reminder that God works in mysterious ways and often has a much larger purpose in mind than we know about. "For who has known the mind of the Lord that he may instruct him?" (1 Cor. 2:16). "'For my thoughts are not your thoughts, neither are your ways my ways,' declares the Lord. 'As the heavens are higher than the earth, so are my ways higher than your ways and my thoughts than your thoughts'" (Isa. 55:8–9).

These words call for faith, which is the gift of God (Eph. 2:8–9)—faith to believe that, "in all things God works for the good of those who love him, who have been called according to his purpose" (Rom. 8:28). God has a purpose, God has all power, and God deserves all praise.

11

NABAL, ABIGAIL, AND DAVID

BIBLE PASSAGE

1 Samuel 25

OBJECTIVES

1. To examine the personalities and actions of Nabal and Abigail.
2. To notice David's spiritual condition at this time.
3. To discuss communication in marriage in the light of this lesson.
4. To discuss loyalty in marriage.
5. To see how God works through people and circumstances to care for His children and work out His plan.

BACKGROUND

David, the young shepherd boy, had been anointed by Samuel to become king of Israel in place of Saul. The Spirit of

God came upon David, and he was remarkably blessed. He was called on to play the harp for moody, depressed King Saul. In this position he gained insights on political and palace life.

David's troubles with Saul began when he killed Goliath and became the national hero. Saul's jealousy grew into uncontrolled fits of rage against David. Everyone, including Saul's son Jonathan and daughter Michal, recognized Saul's injustice. At last, Jonathan and Michal helped David escape Saul's death plot against him, and David hid out in wilderness areas with the band of men who had pledged allegiance to him.

Just before Nabal and Abigail are introduced to us in the biblical narrative, we have the account of another of Saul's skirmishes against David. David rejected the perfect opportunity to kill Saul and instead faced him bravely and tried to reason with him. Saul was shocked into sanity and made peace with David. David, however, was wise enough not to trust Saul and remained in the wilderness areas with his band of men. In all of these trials David stayed close to God, guided by the priest Abiathar. David and his band protected God's people and even saved the whole city of Keilah from the Philistines.

QUESTIONS FOR PERSONAL STUDY

1. *Find five facts about Nabal in 1 Samuel 25:2–3.* More than five can be found:
   — He lived in Maon.
   — He had property in Carmel.
   — He was wealthy.
   — He had 1,000 goats and 3,000 sheep.

— He was shearing sheep in Carmel.
— He had a wife named Abigail.
— He was a Calebite—from the tribe of Judah.
— He was surly and mean.

2. *Why was David in Maon? See 1 Samuel 23:24–29.* This passage tells of the first time David went to this area to escape the pursuing Saul. Now, after another shaky treaty of peace with Saul (1 Sam. 24:16–22), David and his men returned to their best hiding places.

3. *What do we know about David's band? See 1 Samuel 22:1–2.* David's band was composed of loyal family members, debtors, discontented and distressed people, outlaws, outcasts, and fugitives from justice. Before long there were four hundred of them traveling with him.

   Bob sees here a similarity to Christ and His church. Jesus also was criticized for taking in outcasts and sinners and numbering them as His own.

4. *Did David have a right to expect a gift of food from Nabal (1 Sam. 25:7–8, 16, 21)? See Nehemiah 8:10–12.* David and his men were in need of food. Their need should have created a generous response from any fellow countryman, especially one of the same tribe. Add to this the fact that David and his men had protected Nabal's servants and property from attack by roving bands of thieves, and we see that Nabal owed them an appreciative response at least. Nabal would have had no sheep to shear if it had not been for David's protection. The Nehemiah passage and also Esther 9:22 indicate that festivals and feasts were a time for sharing. Sheepshearing was a time of hard work and feasting. There was plenty of food on hand for the occasion. This reminds us of the now almost-legendary threshing feasts in the United States.

5. *Why did Nabal respond as he did (1 Sam. 25:10–11)?*

Was it because of pride, prejudice, politics, or other reasons? Nabal's response could have been motivated by any of these reasons and many others. He was a proud man and a powerful one. He didn't want to part with any possessions if he could avoid doing so. His answer indicates prejudice against the "inferior" people in David's band. His questions about David's identity lead us to believe that he strongly supported Saul as king. David was well-known to everyone in that country, so Nabal's refusal to recognize him indicated refusal to recognize David as the future king, chosen by God.

Bob says Nabal was wicked and selfish and known for his harsh, niggardly dealings with men. He was not about to change his ways for David. The intensity of his ill humor is found in verse 14 where the words "hurled insults" have also been translated "screamed" or "flew at them."

6. *Give at least two reasons why the servants went to Abigail for help (1 Sam. 25:14–17).* Here are some possible answers:
    — They were afraid for their lives.
    — They were ashamed of Nabal's injustice.
    — They warned her of her danger.
    — They knew she would listen and act.
    — They knew of David's power as a commando leader.

7. *Why did Abigail act as she did (1 Sam. 25:17, 26, 30–31)?* These verses give us some insight into her reasoning:
    — She did not want bloodshed.
    — She knew God's laws about personal vengeance.
    — She knew God was with David.
    — She did not want David to sin.

— She believed David would be king.

— She wanted to ally herself with David and God.

8. *Should she have waited for the Lord to intervene? Explain.* In discussing this lesson with other groups, some members have maintained that if Abigail had not acted, but had prayed, she would not have deceived her husband, and the Lord would have diverted David.

Bob, however, believes strongly that God chose to intervene through Abigail. God equips His children with talents, abilities, and intellects for His use in the regulating of events and circumstances. He expects us to think and act in times of crisis. An example of this is found in 1 Samuel 21:10–15: David found himself in danger in Gath, and instead of passively waiting for deliverance, he immediately pretended to be insane and was thrown out of the city into safety. Perhaps even more to the point was God's intervention by using David to kill Goliath.

9. *Did Abigail betray her husband (1 Sam. 25:19, 25–26)?* She saved his life. This involved acting without his consent and recognizing his wicked foolishness. This was not betrayal, it was mercy.

10. *What do you learn about her from her speech in 1 Samuel 25:24–31? Compare it with Joshua 2:8–13.*

— She was humble.

— She took Nabal's blame, but said that if she had known about David's request none of this would have happened.

— She used words well, including the metaphorical reference to the slingshot in verse 29.

— She believed God was on David's side, and she wanted to identify herself with God's chosen one. (Rahab, too, had wanted to be on God's side and be protected.)

— She showed understanding of David's distress and discouragement and acted as his comforter.

— She understood that, as God's chosen one, David must be kept from sin.

— She recognized that sin would be a staggering burden for David. In this we can see her own spirituality and desire to serve God perfectly.

11. *Why did Nabal die (1 Sam. 25:36–39)?* Nabal died because God, the righteous and just avenger, struck him down. Humanly speaking, Nabal was either so angry with Abigail or so frightened when he learned of the near-massacre he had caused that he had a heart attack and stroke and died.

12. *Why did David marry Abigail?*

— *Because she was beautiful and intelligent.* David recognized this and appreciated it. He may have recognized that these qualities would be desirable for his queen-wife.

— *Because she had kept him from sin.* He may have wanted to reward her for this, but that sounds rather conceited on his part.

— *To protect her.* She was vulnerable without a husband. In those days roving bands attacked and carried off unprotected women and their possessions. Also, by aiding David she had committed treason against Saul and could have suffered his revenge. Marriage to David granted her protection, but also peril as can be seen in chapter 30.

— *To gain control of Nabal's property.* Bob and I disagree here. I believe David was canny enough to see a material advantage here. He could have seen it as the Lord's way of providing for him, or he may have felt he had earned a right to this property. Bob feels David was above such motives. He sees the marriage as an act of chivalry by David.

— *Because he loved her.* Perhaps he had come to love and desire her during the month or two after their meeting. We are not told this.

— *All of these.* This is a possible choice.

— *None of these.* Anyone who gives this answer should be encouraged to share his or her thoughts and insights with the group.

13. *Read 1 Samuel 25:21–22 and Psalm 109. Do you think David may have written this psalm at this time? Describe David's spiritual condition at this time.* In 1 Samuel 25:21–22 we see how David's depression and discouragement caused him to take a terrible oath. Apparently our understanding Father in heaven, who knows our weaknesses and remembers that we are dust (Ps. 103:13–14), did not bind him to that oath.

Psalm 109 is one of the imprecatory psalms—not our usual choice for a devotional. No one knows exactly when it was written, but this psalm expresses clearly the despondency of David when, weak and hungry, he received evil for the good that he had done to Saul and to Nabal.

Any of God's children who have experienced betrayal and depression can be comforted by reading this psalm and setting it in the story we are studying. Driven by despair to swear an oath of violence, David was not forsaken by God. God knew his need and met it in the form of a beautiful, God-fearing woman. God kept David from evil, and he praised the Lord for caring and intervening.

14. *Why was this episode important in David's life? See 1 Samuel 25:39 and Romans 12:19–21.* The leaders of God's people must be good examples. (See qualifications

for church leaders in 1 Tim. 3:1–13 and 1 Peter 5:1–4.) God had established laws for vengeance, which was to be meted out not by the person offended, but by the official "avenger of blood" who represented God's justice. These laws may be found in Deuteronomy 19. Bob says, "David was glad that he was stopped by Abigail from 'running before the Lord' or from wresting justice out of God's hands. Instead, he saw God in action against his enemies and was comforted."

QUESTIONS FOR GROUP DISCUSSION

1. *Can two people of opposite natures, as were Nabal and Abigail (1 Sam. 25:3), be happy in marriage to each other?* We have observed the happy marriages of several couples who appear to have opposite natures. But these couples share a belief in the Lord Jesus Christ as their Savior, and He works in their lives. Their happiness rests on this common bond.
2. *First Samuel 25:17, 19, 24, 35, 37 all deal with communication. The following questions deal with this subject:*
    — *Contrast David and Nabal. Why was one approachable and the other not?* Bob says, "It takes wisdom to communicate well. As Abigail said, Nabal was a fool, not wise." I would add to this that Nabal was proud and self-righteous. David was humble and God-righteous. People who are "poor in spirit" do not hold themselves above others. They know they and all other people are sinners before God. A person who is standing on the same level with others is more approachable.

— How should one deal with a mate who will not communicate? In talking this over, we agreed that one's response should not be a matching stubborn silence. Instead, the wise person will talk out trouble spots to, if not with the other person without condemning him/her. An example is this: Instead of saying, "You make me so mad!" it would be more softening to say, "I am very troubled about our lack of understanding on this," or "I wish I understood your feelings and ideas better." Proverbs 25:15 tells us, "A gentle tongue can break a bone."

— What do these verses tell us about timing in communication? Timing is important. A husband watching a football game on TV is not receptive to a wife who turns off the game to tell him about the great blessing she received in her Bible study class. A temper explosion is not conducive to working out difficult problems; a cooling-off period is needed. Abigail knew her husband well and did not try to reason with him when he was unable or unwilling to listen to her.

— Is it right for husbands and wives to conceal important knowledge from each other? This is a difficult question. There are many variables to examples that might be given. Rather than discussing them all, it might be best to come to the conclusion that we must be governed by the law of love. Some confessions may relieve the sinner but hurt someone else. Knowledge of things that "might have been" may cause dissatisfaction. Love—seeking the best for one's partner—should help us decide this matter.

— How can husbands and wives improve communication with each other? Many practical suggestions may be given by group members. To start things off, we suggest these:

— Recognize that good communication takes work and patience but is worth the effort.

— Try to reserve some time each day to talk with each other.

— When things are going smoothly, tell each other how you want to be approached or dealt with when problems arise. For example: A wife may say, "If you have something to discuss with me, I'd appreciate it if you wouldn't bring it up when I'm making supper." Or a husband might say, "Honey, I wish I had your gift of words. But when you tell me your problems, please leave some breaks between sentences so I can respond to you." If these suggestions are made in a kind way at a time of relaxation, they are less threatening.

— Hypothetical situations may be discussed impersonally, giving an opportunity to reveal your thoughts and wishes. For example: "If you ever dented the car, I'd want you to——." Or, "If you'll be late for supper, I wish you'd——." Or, "I read of someone who——."

3. *In your opinion, was alcoholism one of Nabal's problems?* Many commentators focus on Nabal's drunkenness and blame it for his mean disposition. We don't know if he was an alcoholic. Harvest festivals and sheepshearing feasts traditionally were times when people often drank too much. (See Ruth 3:6–7.)

4. *If married to a mate like Nabal, should one accept him/her or try to change him/her?* Certain things must be accepted. However, we can live the Spirit-filled life and pray for God to change our mate or ourselves. The

danger lies in having such a high opinion of our own attributes that we think our mate should be like us in everything.

5. *Is a mate required to support or endorse the partner no matter what he/she does?* Loyalty is an essential ingredient of a good marriage. However, this lesson illustrates that, like Abigail, we must seek the Holy Spirit's guidance and use our intelligence and good moral judgment in these matters so that we may please the Lord. We are each individually accountable to Him for our deeds.

6. *Notice the providential meeting of David and Abigail in the valley (1 Sam. 25:20). Would David have been as receptive to a repentant Nabal as he was to the beautiful Abigail? Explain.* While acknowledging that most men would be influenced by a beautiful woman, Bob believes that God in His providence could have influenced David just as effectively with gifts offered by a repentant Nabal. We are both impressed by the fact that God knew David so well that He chose to use the charm and beauty of a woman to demonstrate His care for David. Feminine charms are exploited in advertising today and are often used to lead men to sin. Here, Abigail's charms were used to lead a man back to righteousness.

7. *Should husband and wife bear each other's blame (1 Sam. 25:24, 28)? Explain.* Perhaps it would help to give a contemporary example. Imagine that your family is leaving the parking lot after a church service. There is a long line of cars waiting to exit. Suddenly, your husband, who is driving, spots an opening in the line of cars, cuts someone off, and roars away leaving a very angry driver behind. The next day you, the wife, meet this angry person in the supermarket. Should you hide in another aisle or meet the person and say, "I'm sorry that in our hurry

yesterday we cut you off. Please forgive us." We believe that often in marriage we have to be peacemakers and healers. God honors us for this and also rewards us if it involves suffering unjustly for His name's sake.

8. *According to 1 Samuel 25:3, 33, Abigail seems almost perfect. Do you agree with this picture, or does verse 25 suggest to you that she may have despised her husband and thus aggravated his problems and personality flaws?* Bob believes she was honest and merely stated the facts. I think there is a tone here which indicates that she might have despised her husband. If his gruffness was caused by an inferiority complex, her attitude of superiority may have made things worse. We hope that she was as wise and tactful when speaking with her husband as she was with David.

9. *What should one do if married to an "impossible" person?* Bob says, "First, be sure you are not at fault and making the problem worse; then keep in mind that with God all things are possible (Luke 1:37). Other passages that may be helpful are 1 Corinthians 7:12–16 and 1 Peter 3:1–9.

10. *Why is this story in the Bible?* Many reasons may be given. One is that we may learn many things from it to apply to our lives. We must point out, though, that the Bible's main purpose is to unfold the plan of salvation. David was an essential part of that plan. We are encouraged when we learn that David, an ancestor and type of Christ, was never forsaken by God, even though he experienced discouragement and temptation. God was always at work in his life. In His all-wise and eternal plan, in all things God works for the good of those who love Him (Rom. 8:28). This promise is made sure for us in Jesus Christ, David's Son, who is King forever and rules

all the forces of earth and heaven. He is unstained, and justice and mercy are in His hand.

Note: The sequel to this fascinating story of David and Abigail is found in 1 Samuel 29–30. Group members may be interested in the fact that David and Abigail had a son (called Kileab in 2 Samuel 3:3 and Daniel in 1 Chronicles 3:1). Of the many sons of David who caused him pain and trouble (e.g., Amnon, Absalom, Adonijah), we do not read of Kileab causing problems. We may possibly attribute this to the fact that he was trained by an intelligent, God-fearing mother.

12

HOSEA AND GOMER

BIBLE PASSAGES

Hosea 1–3; 14; Jeremiah 3:6–20; Malachi 2:10–16

OBJECTIVES

1. To see how the marriage of Hosea and Gomer was an illustration of God's relationship with His unfaithful people.
2. To explore the concept of God as husband and His people as His wife, seeing His emotions and how we are like Him, bearing His image.
3. To examine biblical passages dealing with divorce and separation.
4. To discuss the role of Christians and the church in ministering to those injured by troubled marriages and divorce.
5. To determine proper courses of action to help save a floundering marriage.
6. To stress God's example of mercy and forgiveness, which lead to reconciliation and true happiness.

BACKGROUND

We approached this lesson fearfully, knowing our inadequacy to do it justice. In studying these passages, we were overwhelmed with the nearness of God and the marvel of His gracious, forgiving love for His people. We worked on this lesson on our twenty-fourth wedding anniversary, praising God for the joy He has given us and praying for all His children who are suffering in the absence of this joy. We pray that this lesson may be used in a special way to bring comfort and healing and, hopefully, reconciliation to "fractured families."

Hosea served as a prophet in the northern kingdom of Israel in the years just preceding its fall and captivity. The two kingdoms, Israel and Judah, were experiencing material prosperity. Their enemies declined in power, and Israel no longer felt the need to maintain a standing army. Instead, trade with many parts of the world flourished. This brought in many pagan cultural influences. Economic prosperity and absence of the fear of war made the people feel secure in themselves. The rich grew richer and more self-indulgent, and the poor grew poorer and were cheated of justice. God's people took up the worship of Baal and Ashtoreth, the fertility god and goddess of the Canaanites and Phoenicians. This worship involved cultic prostitution.

In this context, we see how meaningful it was for God to employ Hosea as a living allegory—marrying a prostitute, suffering injustice through her unfaithfulness, and winning her back with tenderness and forgiveness. Names are important in this book. "Baal" means *master,* and Baal is shown to be an oppressive, false husband in contrast to God, the true husband (Hos. 2:16). The children's strange names were used to attract attention and give occasion for Hosea to proclaim God's warnings.

Hosea's love for God's people and his idealistic concept of them as still united under the line of David made him a good messenger of warning and hope. Many parallels can be drawn between Hosea's time and people and the Western world in the twentieth century. This message is relevant for the church today and its component parts—God's people in the context of marriage and family.

QUESTIONS FOR PERSONAL STUDY

1. *What did God ask Hosea to do (Hos. 1:2–9; 3:1–3)?* God told Hosea to marry a prostitute. When their children were born, God had him give them strange names. (Imagine naming your child "Grand Valley" or "Despised" or some other strange name. Everyone would ask why you chose it.) God used these names to provide conversational opportunities for Hosea to bring his message of warning and hope. Hosea was told to find his unfaithful wife, show her love, pay off her debts, and bind her to him in a faithful marriage (Hos. 3).

2. *What did this action represent? See Jeremiah 2:2, 13, 32; Ezekiel 16:8–34; Hosea 1:10–11; 3:4–5.* These passages portray God and His chosen people as husband and wife. They bemoan the adultery of God's "wife" in serving other gods—giving herself to them. They show God's mercy in seeking His people and forgiving them.

3. *Look at the following verses and describe in a few words what God's feeling is in each verse as He reflects upon His unfaithful wife, Israel.*
   — *Jeremiah 2:2*—He nostalgically remembers what a devoted love Israel had at first.
   — *Jeremiah 2:5*—He analyzes His own actions to see if He is to blame.

— *Jeremiah 2:13*—He sees that her sins of forsaking Him and going her independent way are causing the separation.

— *Jeremiah 4:18–22*—Because He sees her bring this upon herself and sees their "home" destroyed, He cries out in anguish and pain.

— *Jeremiah 5:7–9*—He feels she deserves punishment.

— *Hosea 2:8–9*—He feels unappreciated as a provider.

— *Hosea 2:10–11*—He feels jealous and vengeful. He wants to expose her evil and stop it.

— *Hosea 2:13*—He feels forsaken and forgotten.

4. *Do these emotions correspond with human responses?* These are the identical feelings experienced by couples in a broken marriage. Bob says, "We can see and feel God more clearly and closely through these verses because we can see that we are His image bearers. But when our marriages fail, it is because both partners have to deal with their sinful natures. That is why we must be aware of our commitment, our marriage to God. His perfection can atone for our failings and make our marriages secure."

5. *Does God allow or sanction divorce when a mate commits adultery? See Deuteronomy 22:22; 24:1–4; Jeremiah 3:8; Matthew 19:8–9.* Adultery is such a terrible sin in God's eyes that He attaches the death penalty to it in Deuteronomy 22:22. Some people feel that Deuteronomy 24:1–4 suggests the possibility that there are grounds for divorce other than adultery. Others believe this passage is talking about sexual impurity as grounds for divorce. Jeremiah 3:8 shows God Himself granting a divorce, dissolving the marriage bond because of Israel's adultery. In Matthew 19:8–9 Jesus teaches that marital unfaithfulness is the only acceptable grounds for divorce. Nowhere does the Bible teach that a person

must or *should* get a divorce because his/her mate has been unfaithful.

6. *What do we learn about marriage and divorce from Malachi 2:10–16; Matthew 1:19; 5:27–32; 19:3–9; 1 Corinthians 7:10–16?* In Malachi 2, God explicitly says that He hates divorce. He says that a great show of religious zeal will not wipe out the sin of unfaithfulness. Matthew 1:19 inserts a compassionate tone into this discussion. Joseph had pity on Mary, who he thought was unfaithful. He intended to spare her the pain and disgrace of a public divorce. Jesus, in Matthew 5:28, teaches that every unfaithful thought or inclination is adultery. Some modern psychologists suggest that it is perfectly acceptable to fantasize about other people during intercourse in marriage. Jesus would unhesitatingly label these fantasies adultery. First Corinthians 7:10–16 is a difficult passage and has been interpreted in many ways. It seems to allow separation for the sake of peace, but not remarriage. This passage does not seem to sanction divorce. The emphasis is on working for reconciliation, spiritual unity, and peace.

7. *What does God require for reconciliation (Jer. 3:13–14; 4:1–2)?* God calls Israel to acknowledge her guilt, to return, to change her ways. As Bob says, "Repentance, confession, and change of heart are needed. In marriage, reconciliation is possible if both partners will take these steps and draw near to the Lord."

8. *In the example of God and His unfaithful people, the sin is all on one side. Is this true in human marriages?* An old proverb says, "There are two sides to every story," and in human marriage this is true. Usually there is guilt on both sides, but sometimes, especially in cases of adultery, the guilt may belong mainly to one partner. This was true of

the husband who left his wife who had helped him through college and early business years. He said she was no longer youthful and beautiful, and he did not think she helped his "image of success" in the business world, so he divorced her and married an attractive younger woman.

9. *What is the message of Hosea and Gomer's marriage (Hos. 2:16, 19–20)?* This marriage eloquently teaches God's abiding love, mercy, and forgiveness. Submission to the Lord, as to a husband, is a thing of joy. The Lord binds His people to Himself in true happiness. The ingredients of a happy Christian marriage are righteousness, justice, love, compassion, faithfulness and acknowledgment of the Lord (Hos. 2:19–20).

Note: Question 9 may be used to end the group discussion. Stressing ingredients of a happy Christian marriage could end the discussion with a positive note.

QUESTIONS FOR GROUP DISCUSSION

1. *How should Christians respond when they hear that a couple is seeking a divorce?* They should not take sides or gossip about the marriage breakdown. They should pray for the couple and the troubled family. If they are close friends, they should express their genuine love, concern, and sadness and should encourage the couple to get help.

2. *How should Christians respond when they hear that an estranged couple has been reconciled (Luke 15:8–10)?* It is interesting to note in this parable that the woman did not call in her neighbors to mourn with her over her loss. Instead, she went into action herself and looked for the

coin. When she found it, she wanted everyone to share her joy, as the angels do when a sinner repents.

When an estranged couple is reconciled, fellow Christians should rejoice with them, welcome them as a restored unity, and build a positive image of their marriage when telling others about the reconciliation. However, they should not gossip about the "dark days" of the marriage as a contrast to the new joy.

3. *Seeing that God experiences the pain of unfaithfulness and divorce when His people reject Him, how will He deal with His children who suffer this agony in the breakdown of their marriage?* God hates the sin in our lives, and He does not want to see us suffer the inevitable results of it (Jer. 4:19). Yet He understands our hurt and anguish perfectly and comes to minister to us in mercy and love. Jesus came to "bind up the brokenhearted" (Isa. 61:1). He came to free us from the slavery of sin and its results in our lives (Luke 4:18).

4. *How can the church minister to those who have suffered or are suffering through divorce?* The body of Christ should show special love, concern, and care for its injured members. This can be done with prayer, loving notes, conversations, and by including them in the activities of Christian fellowship. Officially, the pastor, elders, and deacons should look after their spiritual and material needs and support them with spiritual counsel and encouragement. Some people believe that those who are divorced should have their own groups for Bible study and fellowship, while others reject this idea and advocate "mainstreaming" them. Much can be said on both sides. But the emphasis should be on accepting them in love and helping them grow spiritually.

5. *If a Christian spouse believes his/her mate is unfaithful,*

how should this situation be handled? Because some divorces have been caused merely by suspicion, we must first recommend that the mate be confronted with the matter, tactfully and lovingly and not with a harsh accusation. Every effort should be made to allow the mate to prove the suspicion false or to repent and seek reconciliation and forgiveness. One of the ingredients of a good marriage is justice tempered with compassion (Hos. 2:19–20).

Matthew 18:15–17 gives some guidelines: Go to the mate personally and privately, hoping for reconciliation. If this is not successful, add the testimony of witnesses. If this does not work, seek the help of the church. If the mate despises the loving discipline of the church, separation is permissible. But we must add that Jesus' teaching in this chapter stresses forgiveness—"seventy times seven" (Matt. 19:21–22).

6. *When should a couple seek marital counseling?* Bob says, "When day-to-day problems fail to be resolved in a reasonable amount of time and when communication has broken down, a couple should seek help." I would add that a couple should get help whenever the peace in the home is seriously threatened.

7. *From whom should a couple seek marital counseling?* Christians must be counseled by Christians—preferably trained and competent pastors or counselors.

8. *Should one marriage partner receive counseling if the other member refuses it?* Though it may make the reluctant partner very angry, we believe that the higher good of healing the marriage calls for counseling even of only one partner. With objective evaluation, the one partner can see him/herself and the need for change and forgiveness on his/her part. Then he/she can learn how to reach and deal with the stubborn partner.

9. *What are some far-reaching results of divorce?* Children of divorced parents suffer emotional problems. They are torn by their loyalties to both parents. Studies show that they are more likely to divorce their partners when they are married. Remarriage practically eliminates the possibility of reconciliation and complicates the emotional struggle by adding more parents and children to be dealt with in the family setting. Friends are lost. Finances cause difficult problems. Society loses stability.

10. *How can Christians help children cope with the divorce of their parents?* Some suggestions are:
    — Give them extra attention so they will not feel forsaken and rejected.
    — Maintain firm, loving discipline.
    — Encourage them to talk out their problems.
    — Get professional help for them if they need it.
    — Do not speak negatively about either parent.
    — Above all, give them love, understanding, and patience.

11. *If a couple is divorced, is the matter finished or should they continue to hope for and work for reconciliation?* The message of this marital allegory (Hosea and Gomer) of God and His wife, the church, is one of continued work and hope for reconciliation. God actively seeks reconciliation, even after Israel divorces herself from Him. Hosea's prophecy has a strong note of hope and the promise of great happiness after reconciliation (Hos. 2:21–23; 3:5; 5:15; 10:12; 11:8–11; 14:1–2, 4). God is a realist, however, and He knows how sin hardens hearts. We find the word "remnant" used many times in the prophets' words—e.g., "A remnant will return, a remnant of Jacob will return to the Mighty God" (Isa. 10:21), indicating that not many will respond. Yet God values

each of His children and each of their marriages and patiently works to bring them to healing and forgiveness.

If, however, the divorced partners marry others, the hope for reconciliation almost disappears. In fact, the Bible frowns on remarriage to the first mate if one has been married to another after divorce (Deut. 24:1–4; Jer. 3:1). This could mean breaking another marriage vow and fracturing another family.

Paul writes: "A wife must not separate from her husband. But it she does, she must remain unmarried or else be reconciled to her husband. And a husband must not divorce his wife" (1 Cor. 7:10–11).

12. *What can we learn from Hosea 2:14–20 and Romans 12:14–21 about how to seek reconciliation?* In the Hosea passage, God becomes a courting lover and renews their love by winning His unfaithful wife to Himself again. He makes her so happy that she doesn't even remember her other lovers.

Bob stresses these important facts drawn from the Romans passage: "We must *forget ourselves and our grievances* and *seek the other person's welfare,* not trying to get revenge for our hurts."

13. *Is true happiness possible when a man and woman are reconciled after the pain of separation or divorce? See Hosea 14.* In the Lord all things are possible. Reconciliation with spiritual renewal can produce far greater happiness than was ever known before. This is true for married couples, and it is true for us as God's people, His bride. We suggest that you read aloud Hosea 14 from the New International Version as you close this discussion.

13

AHAB AND JEZEBEL

BIBLE PASSAGES

1 Kings 16; 17:1–2; 18–19:1–3; 20–22; 2 Kings 9

OBJECTIVES

1. To study the historical background of this case history.
2. To analyze Ahab and Jezebel's spiritual commitment and the way it influenced their behavior.
3. To see God's mercy to undeserving people, to tremble at His wrath, and to rejoice in His justice.
4. To examine the influence of strong-minded husbands and wives.
5. To be horrified and disgusted with Satan's work through this marriage, and to rejoice with relief that God is the victor and vindicator!

BACKGROUND

Ahab was the seventh king of Israel—the northern tribes of the divided kingdom. His contemporary was Jehoshaphat, king of Judah, who carried out a great spiritual revival for his people, leading them back to the worship of the true God. It was said of him, "He did not consult Baals but sought the God of his father and followed his commands rather than the practices of Israel. . . . His heart was devoted to the ways of the Lord; furthermore, he removed the high places and the Asherah poles from Judah" (2 Chron. 17:3–4, 6).

Jehoshaphat's worst mistakes were in foreign relations and diplomacy. He wanted peace and arms limitation so that his country could develop a material prosperity. He sought peace and alliance with Israel and cemented it with a "cultural exchange"—his son married the wicked daughter of Ahab and Jezebel. Jehoshaphat saw the beginnings of the disastrous results of this alliance at the close of his reign.

The setting of this lesson is antithetical. God was at work reforming Judah and protecting the messianic line while His archenemy, Satan, was corrupting Israel, using the apparent peace and détente to make the people lose interest in God's promise.

Satan is no slouch, and the disgusting marriage of Ahab and Jezebel with its degenerative effects upon their nation is proof of his subtle power. We should be warned.

QUESTIONS FOR PERSONAL STUDY

1. *What do we know about Ahab's family background (1 Kings 16:25–28)?* He was the son of wicked Omri, king of Israel. Archeological finds reveal that Omri and his son and grandsons were recognized as powerful kings.

2. *What do we know about Jezebel's family background (1 Kings 16:31)?* Jezebel was the daughter of Ethbaal,

who gained the throne of Sidon or Phoenicia by killing his predecessor. Ethbaal was not only a king; he was also a priest to the goddess Astarte (Baal's wife). This worship involved its faithful followers in cultic prostitution, so it is surprising that Ethbaal named his daughter "Jezebel" which means *chaste* or *virgin*. Her strong religious devotion would not allow her to be that. Jezebel's brothers and sisters were strong, aggressive, evil rulers. Her sister Dido founded the city of Carthage.

3. *When did Ahab rule (1 Kings 16:29)?* Ahab began ruling in the thirty-eighth year of Asa, king of Judah, but most of his reign was opposite that of Asa's son, Jehoshaphat. Ahab ruled for over twenty years.

4. *Over whom did Ahab rule (1 Kings 16:29)?* He ruled over the northern ten tribes, called Israel. His main palace was in the capital, Samaria, but he had a summer palace in Jezreel (1 Kings 21:1; 2 Kings 9:30).

5. *Is there proof of Jezebel's devotion to Baal, the god of her fathers (1 Kings 18:13, 19; 19:1–2)?* She tried to wipe out worship of the true God by killing His prophets. She materially provided for the prophets of Baal—they ate at her table. She swore she would kill God's prophet, Elijah, her most powerful enemy.

6. *Did Jezebel lead her husband away from the true God (1 Kings 21:25–26)?* The Bible states clearly that Jezebel urged her husband on his evil way. He was already evil and serving the Devil, but she helped him along the way by making him promote her false religion. His marriage to her was a blatant violation of God's command recorded in Deuteronomy 7:1–5.

7. *Who had the most power or influence in this marriage— Ahab or Jezebel (1 Kings 16:31–32; 19:1–3; 21:7–16)?* Bob appropriately and vehemently answered this ques-

tion: "This damned (literally) woman Jezebel took the power from her weak, childish husband."

8. *What did the powerful Ben-Hadad alliance demand of Ahab (1 Kings 20:3–6)?* Ben-Hadad demanded that Ahab give him his best wives and children and his silver and gold. We learn here that Ahab had other wives, as most rulers of that day did.

9. *How did Ahab respond (1 Kings 20:4, 7–9, 11)?* It seems that Ahab offered to give Ben-Hadad his wives and children, gold and silver, but did not immediately do this. One wonders if Jezebel knew of this. When Ben-Hadad threatened to search the palace, Ahab was advised to resist. He quoted a proverb which is similar in meaning to ours, "Don't count your chickens before they are hatched" (1 Kings 20:11).

10. *Why was the military campaign a success (1 Kings 20:23, 28)?* The battle was not won because God loved Ahab or because Ahab was such a good military strategist. God was defending the honor of His own name. He proved Himself to be the Lord of all the earth.

11. *Why did the triumphant Ahab make a treaty with Ben-Hadad (1 Kings 20:30–34)?* Ahab followed his own inclinations. He did not seek the Lord's guidance. Bob says, "He was a pushover, a weak ruler, flattered by this seeming humility of his proud enemy." Another key factor was that Ben-Hadad offered the return of conquered properties (which should have been Ahab's anyway because he had now conquered Ben-Hadad), and even more important, he made trade agreements with Ahab.

12. *Do similar things happen in foreign policies today?* Today, too, the alluring prospects of expanded export markets and trade privileges blind leaders to their own weakness in negotiating with an enemy.

13. *What did God think of the clemency shown to Ben-Hadad (1 Kings 20:42)?* Ahab took the credit for the victory, but God had really won the battle and determined that Ben-Hadad should die. Ahab robbed God of a complete victory in which His justice was satisfied by the death of the attacker, so God demanded Ahab's own life in payment. (See footnote in NIV.)

14. *How did Ahab know that Micaiah was not speaking the truth at first (1 Kings 22:16)?* Ahab knew because he knew his own guilt and God's judgment against him because of his sins and his weak handling of the earlier campaign. He did not expect the Lord to grant him success, but he was determined to have his own way.

15. *Name at least three things you learn about Ahab's character from these passages. See especially 1 Kings 20:1–12, 43; 21:1–4, 16.* Bob is impressed with Ahab's weakness and timidity and his sulky childishness. Ahab was cocky and only asked for advice when his weakness led to more trouble. He was easily flattered and duped. He seemed able to ignore his conscience completely, happily taking possession of Naboth's vineyard which Jezebel had obtained in such a despicable way.

16. *What do we know of Ahab and Jezebel's style of living (1 Kings 22:39)? See also Amos 3:15.* They lived in luxury, having summer and winter homes with expensive, imported furniture. A "palace inlaid with ivory" indicates immense wealth.

17. *How did Ahab die (1 Kings 22:34–36)?* O the irony here! Ahab tried to hide from God's judgment by going out to battle in disguise, but God sent a random shot directly into his heart at a joint in his armor. No man can thwart God.

18. *How did Jezebel die (2 Kings 9)?* Jezebel heard that Jehu was coming to destroy her and her family. When she saw

that defeat was inevitable, she put on her make-up and had her hair done. Some believe that she, an old lady, hoped to seduce the young warrior, Jehu, and win his favor. Others believe that she knew she had to die so she wanted to look queenly, especially if she were to lie in state. (Some women might suggest that they can meet any difficult situation more confidently if their hair looks good!)

God did not allow Jezebel any honor in death. Her aides threw her out of a window, and she was trampled to death. The only parts of her body that could be recovered were her skull, her feet, and her hands—all of which were used in the service of sin.

19. *How did the corrupt influence of Ahab and Jezebel lead to the downfall of God's people (1 Kings 22:51–53; 2 Kings 8:25–27)? See also Amos 2:6–16; Micah 6:9–26.* Their children, leaders of God's people, perpetuated their sins and promoted idol worship. The people continued to oppress the poor and to practice cultic prostitution. They rejected and corrupted God's prophets, following the example of Ahab and Jezebel. Because of this, God crushed them and brought them into captivity.

20. *How does the Bible summarize Ahab's life and reign (1 Kings 16:33)?* Ahab is awarded the trophy for doing more to make God angry than all the kings of Israel put together—and they were a bad lot. What a frightening, terrible denunciation!

QUESTIONS FOR GROUP DISCUSSION

1. *What do we mean when we call someone a "Jezebel"?* For many years the term "Jezebel" was used to describe

a woman who wore make-up. This came from the account of Jezebel painting her eyes to prepare for Jehu's arrival. Now the name usually labels a woman as hard, powerful, manipulative, and evil.

2. *Why did Jezebel have so much power over Ahab?* Satan empowered her, and her weak husband was easy prey.

3. *Did Ahab fear God (1 Kings 18:18–20, 41–42, 21: 20–24, 27–29)?* Bob answers, "Ahab was afraid of God as all men are when He confronts them with sin and punishment. But he did not 'fear the Lord' in the sense of reverencing or worshiping Him." Ahab was certainly aware of God's power because he consulted the prophets for God's word. He knew his guilt and the need for repentance. He gave his children Jehovah-based names: "Athaliah" means *strong as Jehovah,* "Ahaziah" means *held by Jehovah,* and "Jehoram" means *he whom Jehovah exalts.*

4. *Why was Jezebel more zealous in her religion than Ahab was in his?* Some people believe women are more zealous in religion than men and that this explains Jezebel's zeal. A better answer is found in the training Ahab and Jezebel received as children. Ahab's father, Omri, was evil and did not worship the God of Israel, so he did not train his son to do so. On the other hand, Jezebel's father was not only a king, but a priest for the goddess Astarte. Jezebel was trained well in the religion of her father. From this, we can see the importance of training our children to serve the Lord so that when they meet other influences in their adolescent and adult lives they will not be overcome by evil.

5. *Can there be true love and harmony in a marriage in which husband and wife are of opposing religions? See Deuteronomy 7:1–5 and 2 Corinthians 6:14–18.* Con-

sider also Ezra 9 and Nehemiah 13:23–27. These Bible passages certainly teach that there can be no marital harmony in the union of a Christian and a non-Christian or one of an opposing faith. These Old Testament passages are almost frightening as they report the severe measures taken against this sin. Mixed marriages are used by Satan to weaken the church. The partners serve and work for opposing masters. They become antagonists. In this day of religious tolerance, it sounds bigoted, unkind, and impolite to point this out. But perhaps Satan subtly uses our religious tolerance as a weapon. Bob adds, "It is sad that God's children are not more emphatic in teaching this, especially when we see the results all around us in broken homes and weakened commitment to God."

6. *Jezebel's zeal for her religion encouraged her husband on his way to eternal death. How can a Christian husband or wife be used to lead his/her mate to Christ? See 1 Corinthians 7:12–16 and 1 Peter 3:1–2.* The Corinthian passage does not endorse marriage as a mission field—in other words, entering marriage with the idea that the Christian mate will "convert" the non-Christian in marriage. This passage does, however, give great encouragement and counsel to the person who finds himself/ herself, as a Christian, married to a non-Christian. In this circumstance, the Christian can call on the power of God to enable him/her to live a life of winning Christian love, believing that the Lord may use this means to save the unbeliever and bless the home.

7. *What responsibility does the stronger-minded husband or wife have to his/her mate?* Each of us has certain strengths which shape our marriage. These must be used to bring out the best qualities in our mate and to help

him/her to grow spiritually, discovering and developing his/her gifts for the Lord. Often one partner is stronger or more assertive than the other, and this strength should be used as a positive, building force. Assertiveness must be changed to service of one for the other. The truly happy, meek person is one whose strength is selfless and used by the Lord (Matt. 5:5).

It must also be pointed out that some apparent weakness is a disguise for manipulative strength. This is true when one says continually, "Poor me, I can't do that," thereby loading extra burdens and responsibilities on another. If one is married to someone who exploits weakness, it would be a loving service to insist that this person take responsibility and encourage him/her to grow in this area.

Bob emphasizes that justice is an important part of a good marriage, and the stronger-minded mate should not be unjust or cruel in dealing with the other.

8. *Who has more influence in the home—husband or wife?* This is an open-ended question which should stimulate much discussion. Many variables may be suggested, such as: in the marriage? in the family? in choosing a home? in making decisions? etc. Also, individual personalities make a difference.

It is valid to point out that a woman has tremendous influence on a man for good or evil and that a mother and full-time homemaker can have a powerful influence on the children and on the social structure of the marriage. This carries a heavy responsibility to use this influence in the service of the Lord.

This observation does not ease the responsibility for the man, however. In the first place, a Christian man is required to choose a Christian wife. And as head of the family, God holds him responsible for the family. He cannot face God's judgment on his marriage and family if he has not been its faithful spiritual leader. As Bob points out, "Homemaking and parenting are the tasks of both husband and wife, though each has his/her own role and unique contribution to the working out of this challenge." We agree that marriage should not be a struggle for power. Instead, we find we are happiest when we are serving one another in love as Christ commanded us through Paul's words (Gal. 5:13).

9. *Did Ahab and Jezebel have a happy marriage? Can you be happily married to someone you despise?* Surely Jezebel must have despised her weak, sullen husband. And Ahab must have hated his wife for her power over him, the king. Also, there is no true happiness apart from God. It seems impossible that these two self-seeking people could have been happy in marriage or in any other part of life.

10. *Ahab and Jezebel were parents of a daughter, Athaliah, who married Jehoram, son of Jehoshaphat, king of Judah. This wicked Athaliah encouraged Baal worship and tried to wipe out the line of David by killing all her grandsons and proclaiming herself queen (2 Chron. 22:10–12). She was not successful, however, and through her marriage to Jehoram, Ahab and Jezebel became ancestors of Christ. What is the significance of this fact? Consider Genesis 3:15 and Revelation 12, especially verses 4 and 5. What comfort can be derived from this?* The Lord uses Christian marriages to build His kingdom. Satan uses marriages in his attempt to tear that kingdom apart. This is the age-old battle that began in the Garden of Eden. The church continues to fight, but the victory has been won by Christ's defeat of Satan.

The study of this disgusting couple ends on a triumphant note: God always wins! No matter how strong the
forces of evil may seem, He has a plan and He has made
promises that He will fulfill. Though many journalists
may write about the death of the family and the demise of
marriage, God does not intend this to happen. He will go
on using Christian marriage to build His church and
bring blessing to those who serve Him.

Note: We cannot close this lesson without reminding ourselves of this danger: we may compare ourselves with Ahab
and Jezebel and conclude that they were so wicked that they
deserved damnation, while we somehow deserve salvation.
We must remember that we all stand condemned before God.
We all have failed at times to serve one another and the Lord
in our marriages. But our merciful God honors even the
weakest repentance (1 Kings 21:27–29). He will take our
confessed sins and failures, as individuals and as married
couples, and renew us in Christ, using us to build and extend
His kingdom. Let us thank Him for guarding the fulfillment of
His promise so that we might be saved.